Contents

A Note About the Author

Sebastian Junger is a writer and a traveler. He has worked as a journalist in the Balkans, Sierra Leone and Afghanistan.

He was born on January 17th, 1962, in Belmont in the state of Massachusetts in the U.S.A. After graduating from Wesleyan University in Connecticut, Sebastian had a job working for a tree company. But after he was injured doing this work, he decided to become a full-time journalist. Sebastian wrote about people who did dangerous jobs. His writing has been published in many different magazines, including *Outside*, *Vanity Fair*, *New York Times Magazine* and *Esquire*.

In 1991, Sebastian Junger was living in Gloucester, a small town on the coast of Massachusetts. He saw houses and properties near his home destroyed by a terrible storm in October of that year. He heard that many fishermen from the town of Gloucester were on their boats during that storm. And one boat, the *Andrea Gail*, disappeared completely.

Two years later, Sebastian decided to write a book about the events that happened in that terrible storm. He spoke to the people of Gloucester. He talked to friends and relatives of the fishermen who had disappeared, and he interviewed members of the rescue services. Many of the people became his friends. And when he wrote his book, *The Perfect Storm*, he thanked all these people for their help.

The Perfect Storm was published in the U.S. in 1997 and it became an international best seller. In 1998, Sebastian and his friends created The Perfect Storm Foundation. This is an organization to help the children of the Gloucester fishermen, and the young people of the town. A successful and exciting film (*The Perfect Storm*) was made from the story in 2000.

SEBASTIAN JUNGER

The Perfect Storm

A True Story of
Men Against the Sea

Retold by Anne Collins

MACMILLAN
MODERNS

INTERMEDIATE LEVEL

Founding Editor: John Milne

Macmillan Guided Readers provide a choice of enjoyable reading material for all learners of English. The series comprises three categories: MODERNS, CLASSICS and ORIGINALS. Macmillan **Moderns** are retold versions of popular and contemporary novels, published at four levels of grading—Beginner, Elementary, Intermediate and Upper. At **Intermediate Level**, the control of content and language has the following main features:

Information Control
Information vital to the understanding of the story is presented in an easily assimilated manner and is repeated when necessary. Difficult allusion and metaphor are avoided and cultural backgrounds are made explicit.

Structure Control
Most structures used in the Readers will be familiar to students who have completed an elementary course of English. Other grammatical features may occur, but their use is made clear through context and reinforcement. This ensures that the reading is enjoyable and provides a continual learning situation for the students. Sentences are limited in most cases to a maximum of three clauses and within sentences there is a balance of adverbial and adjectival phrases. Great care is taken with pronoun reference.

Vocabulary Control
At **Intermediate Level** there is a basic vocabulary of approximately 1600 words. Help is given to students in the form of illustrations which are closely related to the text.

Glossary
Some difficult words and phrases in this book are important for understanding the story. Some of these words are explained in the story, some are shown in the pictures, and others are marked with a number like this: ...[1]. Words with a number are explained in the Glossary.

The Places in This Story

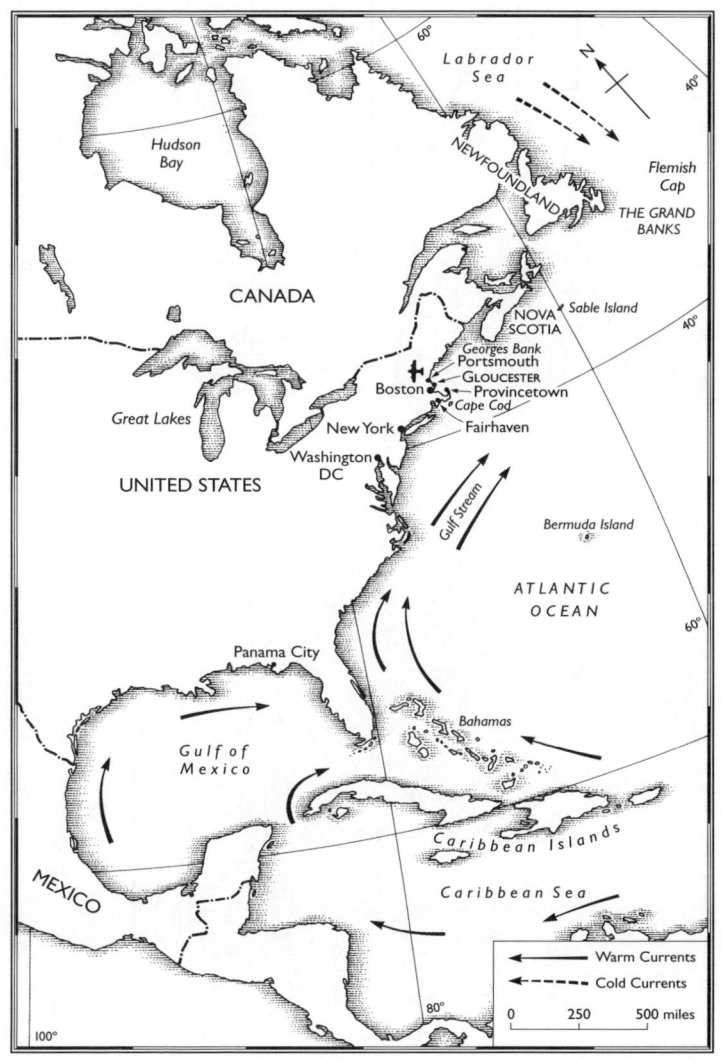

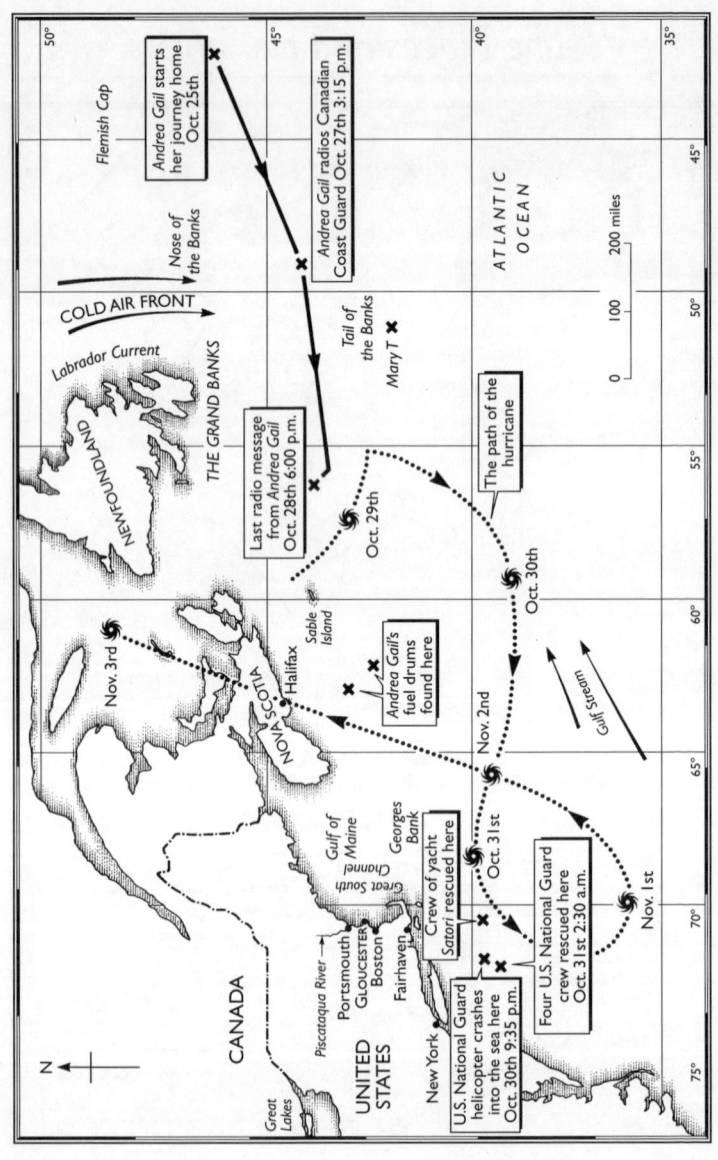

50°

Flemish Cap

Andrea Gail starts her journey home Oct. 25th

45°

Andrea Gail radios Canadian Coast Guard Oct. 27th 3:15 p.m.

Nose of the Banks

ATLANTIC OCEAN

COLD AIR FRONT

Labrador Current

THE GRAND BANKS

Tail of the Banks

Mary T ✕

Last radio message from Andrea Gail Oct. 28th 6:00 p.m.

0   100   200 miles

NEWFOUNDLAND

Oct. 29th

The path of the hurricane

Oct. 30th

Nov. 3rd

Sable Island

Halifax

Andrea Gail's fuel drums found here

NOVA SCOTIA

Nov. 2nd

Gulf Stream

CANADA

Great Lakes

Gulf of Maine

Great South Channel

Georges Bank

Oct. 31st

Nov. 1st

Piscataqua River
Portsmouth
GLOUCESTER
Boston
Fairhaven

Crew of yacht Satori rescued here

Four U.S. National Guard crew rescued here Oct. 31st 2:30 a.m.

UNITED STATES

New York

U.S. National Guard helicopter crashes into the sea here Oct. 30th 9:35 p.m.

N

75°   70°   65°   60°   55°   50°   45°   35°
                                                  40°

Boats, Ships and Aircraft in This Story

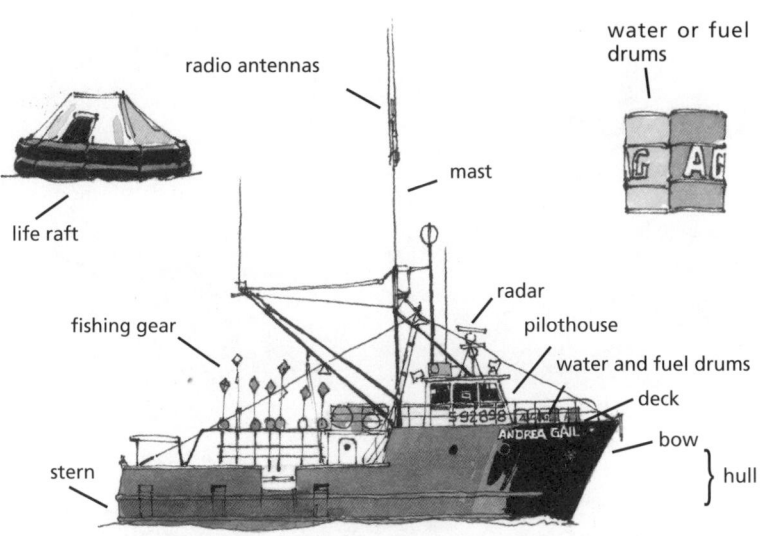

water or fuel drums

radio antennas

mast

life raft

radar

pilothouse

fishing gear

water and fuel drums

deck

bow

stern

hull

swordfishing boat *ANDREA GAIL*

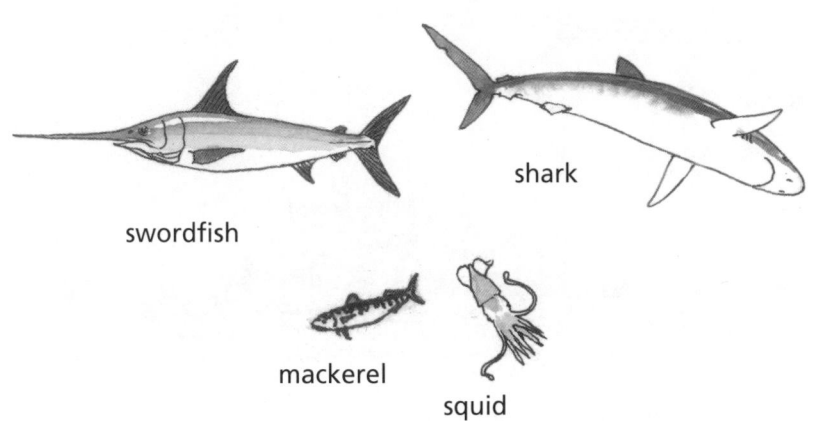

swordfish

shark

mackerel

squid

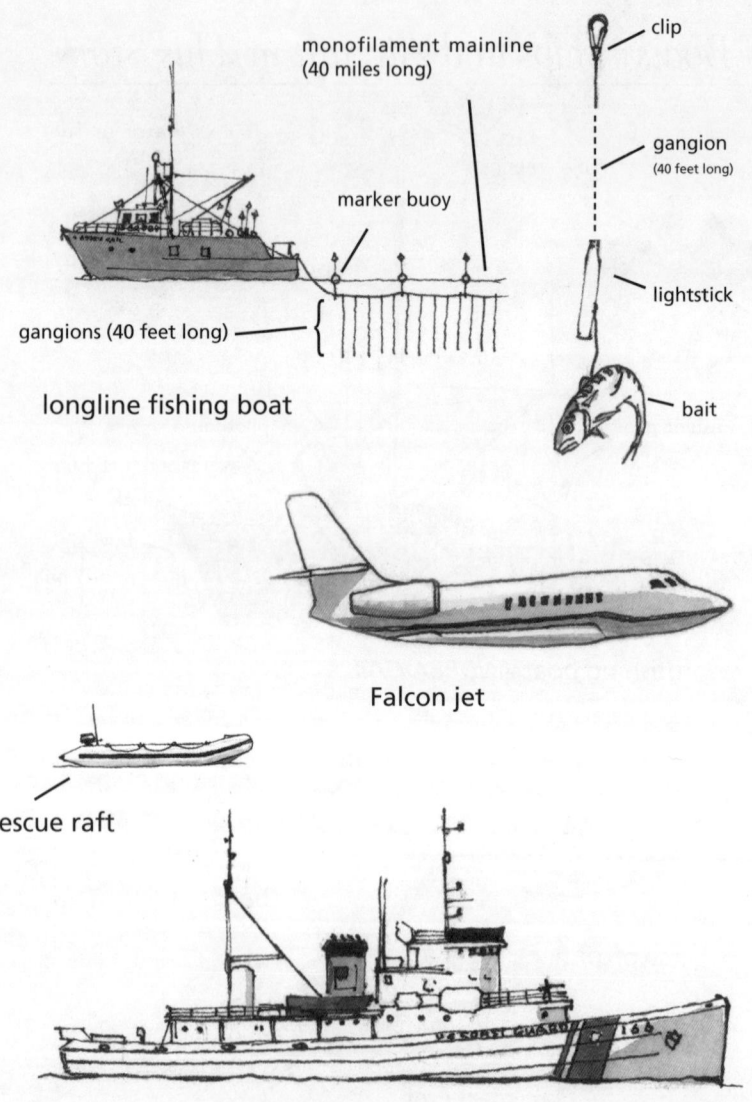

monofilament mainline
(40 miles long)

clip

gangion
(40 feet long)

marker buoy

lightstick

gangions (40 feet long)

bait

longline fishing boat

Falcon jet

rescue raft

U.S. Coast Guard cutter *TAMAROA*

U.S. Coast Guard H-3 rescue helicopter

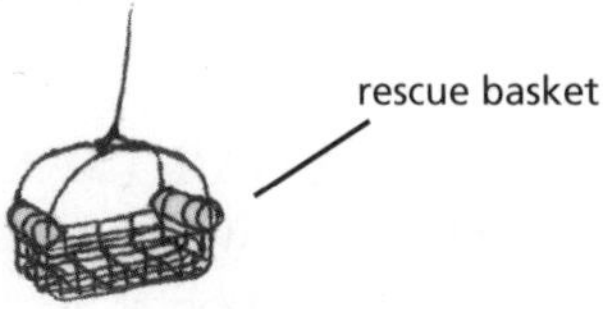

rescue basket

U.S. National Guard H-60 rescue helicopter

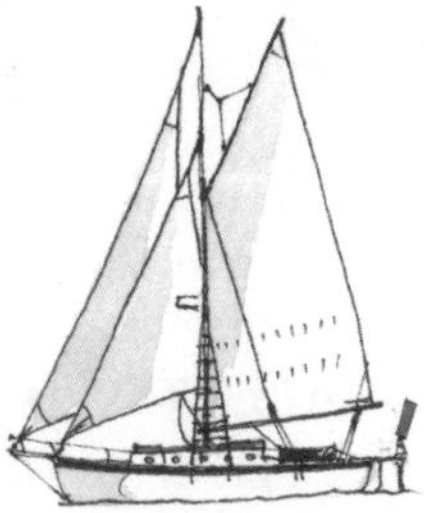

sailing yacht *SATORI*

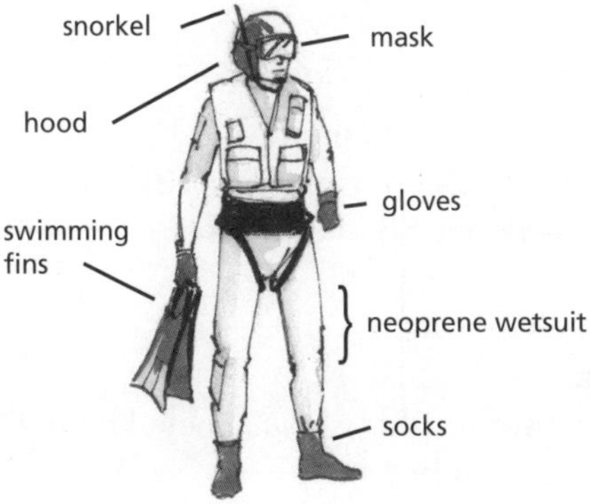

snorkel

mask

hood

gloves

swimming
fins

neoprene wetsuit

socks

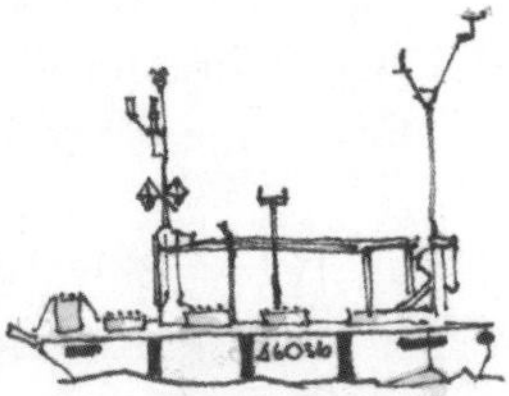

data buoy

U.S. Coast Guard rescue swimmer

The People in This Story

ANDREA GAIL (72-foot swordfishing boat)
Captain: William "Billy" Tyne
Crew: Bobby Shatford
            Michael "Bugsy" Moran
            David "Sully" Sullivan
            Dale "Murph" Murphy
            Alfred Pierre

HANNAH BODEN (swordfishing boat)
Captain: Linda Greenlaw

MARY T (swordfishing boat)
Captain: Albert Johnston

ALLISON (swordfishing boat)
Captain: Tommy Barrie

TERRI LEI (tunafishing boat)

The "Crow's Nest" bar
Ethel Shatford—Bobby Shatford's mother
Chris (Christina) Cotter—Bobby Shatford's girlfriend
Mary Anne Shatford—Bobby Shatford's sister

————

Jodi Tyne—Billy Tyne's ex-wife
Billy Tyne's girlfriend
Bob Brown—owner of swordfishing boats, including the
Andrea Gail and the *Hannah Boden*
Susan Brown—wife of Bob Brown

Doug Kosco—a fisherman who didn't sail on the *Andrea Gail* on September 20th, 1991
Adam Randall—a fisherman who wouldn't sail on the *Andrea Gail*
Debra Murphy—Murph's ex-wife
Dale Murphy—Debra and Murph's 3 year-old son

TAMAROA (205-foot U.S. Coastguard rescue cutter)
Commander: Lawrence Brudnicki

U.S. Coastguard H-3 helicopter
Pilot: Claude Hessel
Rescue swimmer: Dave Moore

U.S. National Guard H-60 helicopter
Pilots: Dave Ruvola
                     Graham Buschor
Engineer: Jim Mioli
Rescue swimmers: John Spillane
                     Rick Smith

***SATORI* (32-foot sailing yacht)**
Captain and owner: Ray Leonard
Crew: Karen Stimpson
                     Sue Bylander

U.S. National Weather Service headquarters, Boston
Chief meteorologist: Bob Case

Gloucester, 1991

*T*his is a true story about a terrible storm. The storm happened at the end of October 1991. It happened over the Atlantic Ocean, not far from the east coast of North America.

Many of the people who were caught in[1] the storm were experienced fishermen. These people had worked on fishing boats for many years and they knew the sea well. Most of them had been caught in bad storms before. But the storm of October 1991 was the worst that any of them had ever seen.

At sea, one boat sank and was never seen again. The storm badly damaged several other boats and their equipment too. It even destroyed a helicopter. But the storm also destroyed homes and property on the land.

Some people died in the storm. Other people's lives were changed forever.

The phrase "a perfect storm" is used by meteorologists[2]. When they talk about a perfect storm, they don't mean that the storm is a very good storm. They mean the opposite of that—they mean that the storm could not be any worse. Fortunately, this kind of storm is very unusual. A perfect storm happens maybe only once in a hundred years.

This book, written in 1997, is the story of the perfect storm of October 1991. It is also the story of some of the people who were caught in that storm. Some of these people were lucky, others were not.

The town of Gloucester, Massachusetts, is north of Boston, on the east coast of the U.S. It takes about forty-five minutes to drive from Boston to Gloucester.

Gloucester is a fishing town. Most of the people who live in the port have jobs connected with fishing. They make their money from fishing, or from doing things which the fishing people need to be done.

The smell of the ocean is very strong in Gloucester, but the ocean there is not very beautiful or romantic. The water in the town's harbor is full of empty beer cans and pools of diesel fuel from boat engines. You can see the fishing boats, tied with ropes to the pier[3], rocking backwards and forwards in the harbor. You can hear the sounds of sea birds, calling noisily to each other. And you can hear men shouting to each other on the boats as they unload the fish that they've caught. These men's clothes are covered with fish blood.

There is a street in Gloucester called Rogers Street. On Rogers Street there is a small hotel called the Crow's Nest[4]. The Crow's Nest hotel is very popular with young fishermen. It's a warm and friendly place, and the rooms there are cheap. Most of the older fishermen have their own homes, where their families live. But many of the younger fishermen don't have their own homes. For these young men, the Crow's Nest is their home between fishing trips.

A woman called Ethel Shatford works in the Crow's Nest. She serves the fishermen drinks and she makes huge pots of fish soup for them. Ethel has lived all her life in Gloucester, in a house about half a mile from the Crow's Nest. She has worked at the hotel since 1980. She comes from a family of fishermen and she understands fishermen and their way of life. Ethel has six children—four sons and two daughters. Her sons have all worked as fishermen and her daughters' boyfriends are all fishermen too.

Ethel is a good, kind woman. She looks after the young

13

fishermen like a mother. Sometimes the fishermen have problems. Maybe they are getting a divorce[5], or maybe they have money troubles. Ethel always finds them a room at the Crow's Nest, and she makes sure that they are OK. Whatever their problems are, at least the fishermen have a good place to stay until they go back to sea[6].

———

This story really begins on the morning of September 20th, 1991. On that morning, Ethel Shatford's son Bobby was lying asleep in an upstairs room in the Crow's Nest. Bobby had light brown hair, a thin face, and a long thin body. He was lying on a wide bed, under a sheet. Beside the young man lay his girlfriend, Christina Cotter. Christina, who was usually called Chris, was an attractive woman in her early forties. She had red-blond hair and a strong, narrow face.

Bobby and Chris's room was very untidy. There was a TV standing on a cupboard in one corner. In another corner there was a chair with a plastic seat, which was covered with marks from burning cigarettes. There were beer cans and empty food packets lying around on the floor. Bobby's large bag lay on the floor too, with his T-shirts and blue jeans spilling out of it.

At eight o'clock Bobby woke up. Outside, the autumn rain was falling softly. Bobby had a lot of things to do and not much time to do them in. In a few hours, he was going on a month-long fishing trip. He was going to spend four weeks on a boat called the *Andrea Gail*. The *Andrea Gail* was going to head out[7] to an area of the North Atlantic Ocean which was called the Grand Banks. There were usually plenty of fish out at the Grand Banks fishing grounds[8].

Soon after Bobby woke up, Chris woke up too, and they

went downstairs to the bar where Bobby's mother, Ethel, was already working. Another fisherman was in the bar—a friend of Bobby's named Bugsy Moran. Michael "Bugsy" Moran had long, wild hair and sometimes he behaved in a crazy way. Like Bobby, he was now a member of the *Andrea Gail*'s crew. He and Bobby were going to work together on the boat.

"Hi, Bugsy," said Chris. "Would you like to eat breakfast with us?"

Chris, Bobby and Bugsy drove across town in Chris's car to have breakfast in a café called the White Hen Pantry. An hour later, when they returned to the Crow's Nest, they found a third member of the *Andrea Gail*'s crew there. This man was named Dale Murphy, but most people didn't call him Dale. They used his nickname[9], which was "Murph." Murph was a huge man with thick black hair and a thin beard. He looked like a bear.

Murph was divorced. His ex-wife, Debra, lived in Florida with their three-year-old son, who was also called Dale. Murph loved his little son very much and was always thinking about him.

"I want to get some toys for Dale before we leave port," he said to Chris.

"OK," said Chris. "I'll drive you to the shopping center[10] by Grand Harbor Beach."

So the three men—Bobby, Bugsy and Murph—got into Chris's car and she drove them to the shopping center. They went into a large store. While Bobby and Bugsy bought some warm clothes for their trip, Murph walked through the toy department, filling a shopping cart with toys for his son. When they had all finished shopping, they drove back to the Crow's Nest. Then they sat quietly in the bar, drinking beer.

Another fisherman was in the bar.

A little later, Bobby's sister, Mary Anne Shatford, came into the bar. Bobby loved Mary Anne, but he was a little afraid of her too. She was older than Bobby and she always told him what to do. He knew that she would be angry if she saw him drinking beer in the morning. So he tried to hide the beer bottle behind his arm. But he was too late, Mary Anne had seen it.

"You shouldn't drink beer so early in the day, Bobby," she said.

Mary Anne looked angrily from Bobby to Chris. Usually, Chris and Mary Anne were good friends, but Mary Anne hadn't been very happy with Chris lately. She thought that Chris allowed Bobby to drink too much.

Bobby didn't say anything at first. Then he replied quietly.

"Chris loves you, Mary Anne," he said. "I love you, too."

Mary Anne was very surprised. Bobby had never said anything like that to her before. Why was he saying it now? She stared at her brother for a moment, then she turned and went out of the bar.

———

Chris Cotter was very much in love with Bobby Shatford. Although she had often seen him around the town, she had never really talked to him until the previous New Year's Eve. That evening—on December 31st, 1990—there had been a big party in the town. Bobby and Chris had met in the Crow's Nest and had started talking. Then they had gone to the party together. Soon after that they were meeting each other all the time. And one evening, Bobby got down on his knees in front of Chris and asked her to marry him.

"Yes, of course I'll marry you!" she shouted excitedly.

They had started to plan their future life together. But

there were some problems. Chris was divorced and she had three children. Bobby was separated[11] from his wife, although they weren't divorced yet. They had two children, who lived with Bobby's wife, and Bobby gave her money every month to look after them. But his wife had complained that Bobby didn't pay her enough money for child support[12].

Bobby's wife hired[13] a lawyer. At the court, the judge agreed with her complaint. The judge decided that Bobby now had to pay his wife more money every month for child support. And Bobby also had to pay his wife extra money for the time before she made her complaint. He had to pay some of this money immediately. The judge said that, if Bobby didn't pay it, he would go to jail.

Ethel gave Bobby some money to pay his wife. And later, when Bobby was alone with Chris, he'd told her some news.

"Listen, Chris, I can get a job on the *Andrea Gail*," he said. "She's one of the best fishing boats on this coast and her new captain, Billy Tyne, is a friend of my family's. The *Andrea Gail* always catches a lot of fish, and the fishermen who work on her make a lot of money. If I go on seven or eight trips with the *Andrea Gail*, I can pay my wife all the money I owe her for child support. It will take about a year, but then I'll be free. I'll get a divorce and we'll be able to start our new life together."

"That's good," Chris had said. "How long does a trip on the *Andrea Gail* last? How long will you be away each time?"

"A trip lasts about thirty days," Bobby had told her.

"Thirty days!" Chris had said sadly. "You can't go away for thirty days! That's too long! I love you, Bobby. I hate it if I don't see you for even half a day!"

But Bobby knew that working as a fisherman on the

Andrea Gail was the only answer to his money problems. So in August 1991, he went on his first trip with the boat. Chris had no way of knowing exactly when he would come back. She felt nervous and worried all the time.

In late August there was a bad hurricane[14] further up the coast. Hurricanes are always called by the names of people, and this one was called Hurricane "Bob."

When Chris heard about Hurricane Bob, she became very frightened. She went to Ethel Shatford's house and watched the Weather Channel[15] on TV for hours and hours. Hurricane Bob caused a lot of damage and destroyed many trees and houses along the coast. Chris waited for the phone to ring. She waited for someone to call with bad news about the *Andrea Gail*. But there was no bad news about any fishing boats, so finally Chris went home.

At last, one night in early September, the phone rang in Chris's apartment. It was Billy Tyne's girlfriend, a pleasant woman who Chris had met before the trip started. Billy's girlfriend was calling from Florida.

"Hi, Chris," she said. "I've got some great news. The *Andrea Gail* is coming back into Gloucester tomorrow night. I'm coming up to meet Billy. I'm flying to Boston tomorrow. Will you pick me up from Logan Airport?"

Chris was very happy and excited. She very much wanted to see Bobby again after their month apart. The next evening, she drove to Logan Airport in Boston and picked up Billy's girlfriend. While she was gone, the *Andrea Gail* arrived in Gloucester harbor. And when Chris got back to the Crow's Nest, Bobby was already there, waiting for her. Chris ran to him and wrapped her arms around him. She held on to him for twenty minutes and wouldn't let him go!

That night, the bar at the Crow's Nest was a very happy place. The fishermen were home safely, and they were with the people that they loved. And Bobby Shatford had become a member of the crew of the *Andrea Gail*—one of the best fishing boats on the east coast of North America.

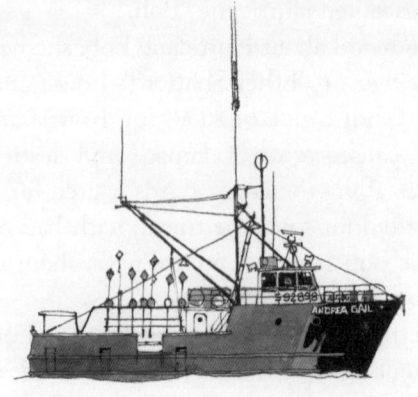

2

Preparing to Leave

The *Andrea Gail* was a swordfishing boat. Sometimes her crew caught other kinds of fish too—sharks for instance—but mostly they caught swordfish.

Swordfish are very dangerous. They are large and strong, and they can weigh up to 500 pounds. But the most unusual and dangerous thing about this fish is its "sword." This is a long thin piece of bone which grows out of the fish's jaw, above its mouth. The sword is a sharp, powerful weapon, like the swords that people once used for fighting.

Swordfish mostly use their swords to attack smaller fish. Small fish swim closely together in huge groups for safety. The swordfish swim through them and tear them to pieces with their sharp swords. But sometimes, swordfish have attacked boats. They can make a hole in the hull of a boat with their swords, so that water comes in. These fish have even attacked fishermen and pulled them from their boats into the sea.

Swordfishing boats like the *Andrea Gail* are called "long-liners." This is because their main fishing line, or mainline, is very long. This monofilament line[16] can be 40 miles long.

Swordfish eat at night. So every evening, fishermen on the swordfishing boats attach pieces of line, called "gangions," all along the mainline. These gangions are about 40 feet long, and each one has a clip at one end to fix it to the mainline. On the other end of each gangion is a large hook, and, just above the hook, a lightstick[17]. On these hooks, the fishermen attach fish bait, which is usually squid, or sometimes

21

mackerel. This food, and the light from the lightsticks, will attract the swordfish during the night. When the mainline is baited, the fishermen put it into the water.

During the night, the swordfish come to the lights on the gangions and they try to take the bait off the hooks. But when a fish tries to take the bait, its mouth becomes caught on the hook and it can't get free. In the morning, the fishermen haul[18] the mainline back into the boat. They take the fish that they've caught off the hooks. They cut the heads and tails from the fish and they cut open their bodies. Then the men put ice inside the bodies and they store the fish— their catch—in the fish hold[19].

During the North American summer, the swordfish are mostly found at the Grand Banks fishing grounds, so the swordfishing boats follow them there. In winter, the fish swim south to the warmer waters of the Caribbean Sea, and the boats follow them there too.

Swordfishing boats make eight or nine trips a year. They are big boats, so they hold a lot of fish and they make a lot of money. Often the boats are away for a month. When a boat comes home to port, the crew stays on shore for a while— maybe a week. The men spend time with their families and they repair their boat. But they never stay in port for very long. As soon as their boat is repaired, they head back out to sea again, to look for more fish.

———

When the *Andrea Gail* returned to port after Bobby Shatford's first trip on her, she brought 15 tons of swordfish back to Gloucester. She was going to stay in port until September 20th, then she would be going back to sea.

The owner of the *Andrea Gail* was a man named Bob

Brown. He owned four other swordfishing boats too. Bob Brown sold the *Andrea Gail*'s catch of fish for $141,582. He sold it to a company called O'Hara Seafoods. Then he divided up the money.

First, he deducted the boat's expenses for the trip—he took away the amount of money that had been spent on equipment for the boat. After that, he took about half of the remaining money for himself. This left just over $53,000. From this amount, Bob Brown deducted the money that had been spent on expenses for the crew. For example, the crew's food and the special clothing they used for working with the fish. Then he divided the rest of the money among the members of the crew.

Six men had gone on the fishing trip—the *Andrea Gail* always had a crew of six. Billy Tyne, the captain, got the largest share of the money. The rest was divided among the other five crewmen. But the older, more experienced men on the boat got more money than Bobby. This had been Bobby's first swordfishing trip, and he didn't know much about sword-fishing yet.

The crews of swordfishing boats can earn very good money. They enjoy earning money, but they enjoy spending it too. Their jobs are difficult and dangerous, and they are away at sea for many weeks of each year. So when the men come home and receive their pay, they want to spend it as quickly as possible. This is especially how the young, single fishermen behave. Sometimes these men spend hundreds of dollars in one night, mostly on drink or women. They do this because they know that soon they will have to go back to sea.

"Fishing is a young man's life—a single man's life," Ethel Shatford, Bobby's mother, often said. She meant that only young men without wives and children should do the job.

But Bobby Shatford was different from the other young fishermen. He had dreams about the future. He wanted to solve his money problems so that he could marry his girl-friend, Chris Cotter. The judge had decided that Bobby had to pay his wife a lot of money. He couldn't marry Chris until all the money was paid. So a job on the *Andrea Gail* was the best answer to Bobby's problems.

After Mary Anne Shatford had left the Crow's Nest, on the morning of that September 20th when this story begins, Bobby and Chris had a few more drinks. Then they, too, left the bar and went out into the soft gray light of the rainy Gloucester day.

They drove across town to a place called Sammy J's. They went there to eat lunch. Bobby ordered his favorite food—fishcakes[20]. As he ordered the meal, he was thinking that this was the last time he would eat fishcakes until the boat returned to Gloucester. When fishermen are at sea, they never want to eat fish!

When Bobby and Chris had finished eating, it was early afternoon. And it was still raining. They went back to the Crow's Nest and picked up Bugsy Moran. Then they drove to the harbor. Bobby and Bugsy wanted to store their bags on the *Andrea Gail*. They also had some work they wanted to do on her.

The boat was tied up to the pier with some other fishing boats. Bobby and Bugsy got out of the car, ran along the pier, and jumped down on to the *Andrea Gail's* deck.

Chris sat in the car, waiting. While she was waiting, she saw a young man coming towards her, carrying a bag. She

The boat was tied up to the pier with some other fishing boats.

knew the man. He was a fisherman named David Sullivan, whose nickname was "Sully". Sully didn't usually work on the *Andrea Gail*, so Chris was very surprised to see him.

"Hi, Sully," she said. "What are you doing here? Are you going on this trip too?"

"Yes," replied Sully. "Billy Tyne called me at home an hour ago. He said that he needed another member for his crew. One of his usual crewmen refused to go on the trip, so Billy asked me to take the man's place. Where's Bobby, Chris? Is he already on board the *Andrea Gail?*"

"Yes," said Chris. "He's already on board."

Suddenly they heard the sound of shouting coming from the *Andrea Gail*. When they turned to look at the deck, Sully and Chris saw Bobby and Bugsy having an argument. Bobby was holding a jug and Bugsy was trying to take it from him. Both men were very angry and they looked as if they were going to hit each other. But after a minute, they became quiet again. They glared[21] at each other, then they both turned and went back to work.

"I don't believe it," said Sully. "These men have to spend thirty days together on a boat, and they're having a stupid argument already."

———

Captain Billy Tyne had had a lot of problems that day. Although he was a very experienced captain, this was only his second trip with the *Andrea Gail* and it was not starting very well.

None of the other five members of his crew wanted to go back out to sea. It was already September 20th, which was quite late in the fishing season. It was difficult to find good men who were willing to go fishing in the North Atlantic at this time of year. Most of them wanted to stay on shore with their wives or girlfriends, drinking beer and enjoying themselves.

Billy knew that Bobby Shatford *did* want to go back to sea because he needed the money. But another crew member, Alfred Pierre, was giving Billy some problems. Alfred was a huge, kind Jamaican man who had lived in New York most of his life. Alfred was still in the Crow's Nest with his girlfriend.

"One minute he says that he wants to come on the trip. The next minute he says that he *doesn't*," Billy Tyne thought angrily. "He's been behaving like this all day because he wants to stay with his girlfriend. And Bugsy Moran is in a bad mood[22] because he doesn't have a girlfriend. And Murph is feeling sad because he's thinking about his son."

But the worst thing for Billy had happened earlier that morning. The sixth member of the crew would have been a man named Doug Kosco. He had been on the previous trip. But that morning, Doug had told Billy that he didn't want to go out on the *Andrea Gail* this time. He didn't give a special reason—he just said that he didn't want to go. So Billy had made a few phone calls to other fishermen that he knew. He'd tried to find a man to replace Kosco. Before he'd finally thought of Sully, he talked to a man named Adam Randall.

Adam Randall was thirty years old and he looked like a rock star. He was very handsome, with long blond hair. He knew most of the other members of the *Andrea Gail's* crew. He had fished all his life and he knew a lot about fishing boats. When he saw a boat, he knew at once if it was safe or not.

Adam had driven to Gloucester that morning with his

father-in-law[23]. He'd walked around the deck of the *Andrea Gail* for a long time, not saying very much. Then finally he had got off the boat and gone back to his father-in-law's car.

"I'm not going out on that boat," he'd said. "I'm not going to take this job."

"What are you saying?" asked his father-in-law in surprise. "You really need this job, Adam. You haven't worked in three months and you need the money. What's the problem? The *Andrea Gail* is a very good boat—it's one of the best sword-fishing boats on the coast."

"I know that," replied Adam. "But I've got a strange feeling about the *Andrea Gail*. When I was walking around her, I felt a cold wind on my skin. I think that none of her crew is going to come back from this trip."

Adam's father-in-law was very shocked.

"Are you going to tell them what you think?" he asked.

Adam thought for a while.

"No," he said at last. "I can't do that. I can't tell them that they're going to die. And maybe I'm wrong. Each man has to make up his own mind[24] about a fishing trip."

So Adam and his father-in-law had driven away.

Billy Tyne wasn't pleased. Now he had to find somebody else very quickly. It was then that he'd remembered Sully.

Sully was twenty-eight years old and he was a very experienced swordfisherman. Also, Sully had a very good reputation[25] among the fishermen. A few years before, a boat he was working on had been in a bad accident at sea, and Sully had saved the lives of several members of the crew.

"Sully's a good man to have on a trip," thought Billy. "People like him because they think that he's lucky."

So Billy called Sully at home, and Sully agreed to go on

the trip. He packed his bag and called all his friends.

"I won't be home for a while," he told them. "I'm going away for a month's swordfishing on the *Andrea Gail.*"

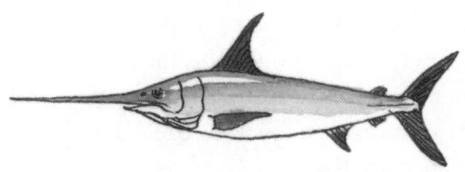

3

Saying Goodbye

When Sully went on board the *Andrea Gail*, Billy Tyne met him on the deck and gave him $4,000.

"Go to the supermarket and buy the food for our trip," Billy said. "Take Murph with you to help."

When fishermen need to buy food for a month's trip out at sea, they don't shop like most people.

Sully and Murph drove a truck to the Cape Ann Market, a big supermarket on Route 127. They each collected a shopping cart, then they walked up and down the store, throwing armfuls of food into their carts.

First they grabbed 50 loaves of bread from the shelves— enough to fill their two carts. They left these carts at the back of the store and brought two more. Then the two fishermen took 100 pounds of potatoes, 30 pounds of onions, and 25 gallons of milk from the shelves. They grabbed huge amounts of cakes, eggs, peanut butter, meat, cereal, spaghetti, ice cream, and frozen pizzas[26]. They also took 30 cartons of cigarettes. The only thing that they didn't take was fish!

Every time Sully or Murph filled a cart, they pushed it to the back of the store and took another one. The other shoppers in the store stared at them, then got out of their way.

When the two fishermen had filled more than twenty carts, they went to the checkout counters[27] to pay.

The store opened two counters especially for them. But it was nearly half an hour before they got their bills. The total came to just under $4,000—nearly all the money that Billy had given Sully.

Every time they filled a cart, they pushed it to the back of the store and took another one.

Sully and Murph loaded all their purchases—all the things they had bought—onto their truck and drove back to the *Andrea Gail*. They carried the purchases, bag by bag, onto the boat. Bugsy and Bobby helped them. They put some of the food down in the fish hold at the bottom of the boat. The rest of the bags were stored in the galley[28].

The *Andrea Gail* had a small refrigerator in her galley. But in her fish hold she had 20 tons of ice. On the way out to the fishing grounds, this ice kept the men's food and the fish bait fresh. Then it kept the catch of swordfish fresh until the boat arrived back in port.

Ice is very important in the business of fishing. Ice can keep fish fresh for weeks, so the fishing boats can stay at the fishing grounds for a long time. This is the way that large quantities of fresh fish get from the oceans to the markets.

Smaller fishing boats have to buy their ice from ice companies. But the *Andrea Gail* didn't need to buy ice from a company. She was a large boat and she had her own ice-making machine. So the crew could make all the ice they needed, before and during a trip.

The *Andrea Gail*'s ice machine was on a raised area called the whaleback deck[29]. More than 30 large metal drums containing fuel or water were also kept on the whaleback deck.

———

Soon the *Andrea Gail* was ready to leave port. The food and the fish bait were stored away in the hold, the fuel tanks and the water tanks were filled, and extra drums of fuel and water were tied to the whaleback deck. The engine was working well and there were no problems—at least, there were no problems with the boat. But Bobby Shatford and Bugsy Moran were still not speaking to each other, because of their argument.

Bobby climbed off the *Andrea Gail* and walked across to Chris Cotter's parked car. Then they drove back across town to Chris's apartment and they lay on the bed there, talking quietly and smoking cigarettes.

Chris and Bobby couldn't see the ocean from the bed, but they could smell it through the open window. And outside, the rain was still falling softly.

Bobby and Chris lay on the bed for about an hour. They were trying to forget that it was Bobby's last day on shore. They were trying to forget that he had to go away in a few hours.

Suddenly the phone rang. It was Sully, calling from the Crow's Nest.

"It's five o'clock, Bobby," he said. "It's time to go."

Bobby and Chris drove slowly back to the Crow's Nest. The other crew members were already there, but everybody was in a bad mood. None of the men wanted to go back out to sea.

Alfred Pierre was still in a room upstairs with his girlfriend and he wouldn't come out. Billy Tyne had just had a two-hour phone conversation with his ex-wife, Jodi, and his two little daughters. He was upset because he hadn't seen his daughters for a long time, and now he was going out to sea again.

Murph was packing toys into a box for his little son. Sully and Bugsy were talking quietly together in a corner of the room, but they weren't looking very happy. Bobby's mother, Ethel, was in a room behind the bar, crying. She was worried about Bobby going away for a month at this time of year.

Bobby went to her. He put his arms around her and tried to make her feel better.

"Don't cry, Mom," he said. "I'll be fine. I'll be home again soon."

"Oh, Bobby, you're going to the Grand Banks," said Ethel. "It's almost October. It's very late in the year to be going out to the Banks. There are lots of storms out there at this time of year. I'll be worried about you."

At last, Alfred Pierre and his girlfriend came downstairs and sat in the bar. Alfred held a bottle of beer in one hand and spoke quietly to his girlfriend. His girlfriend's eyes were red from crying.

Murph finished packing the toys for his son.

"Can you drive me across town?" he asked Chris. "I want to pick up some movies for the trip."

There was a VCR[30] on the *Andrea Gail*, and a fisherman from another boat had said that he'd give Murph some videos.

"Sure, I'll drive you, Murph," Chris replied. "Let's do it now. We don't have much time."

"I don't want to go on this trip," Alfred was telling his girlfriend. "I don't want to go."

In their corner of the bar, Sully was saying the same thing to Bugsy.

"I've got a bad feeling about this trip," he said. "If I didn't need the money, I wouldn't go."

———

Ten minutes later, Chris and Murph returned with a box full of videos.

"OK, you guys," said Billy Tyne. "Let's have one last drink."

The men had a last drink, and then another last drink! Bobby and Chris were standing close together. They were holding hands but they weren't saying very much. Sully came over to them. He knew that Bobby and Chris were in love and that they didn't want to leave each other. He felt sorry for them.

34

"Will you two be OK?" he asked quietly.

"Yes," said Chris. "We'll be fine." Then suddenly she added, "No, I'm not really sure—no, I don't think that we *are* OK, Sully."

Everybody in the bar was thinking the same thing. Six men were leaving Gloucester for a month, and nobody knew if they would return. Ethel went to each of the men and put her arms around them.

"Can we take the color TV from the bar with us?" Bobby asked her.

"Yes," Ethel replied, "if it's OK with Billy."

"They can take the TV, Ethel," Billy said, "but if they watch it instead of doing their work, I'll throw it overboard. I'll throw it off the *Andrea Gail*, into the ocean!"

"That's fine, Billy," said Ethel, laughing. "That's fine."

It was too late now for any of the crew to refuse to go on the trip. Billy Tyne, Alfred Pierre, David Sullivan, Michael Moran, Dale Murphy, and Bobby Shatford were all going to the Grand Banks on the *Andrea Gail*.

"OK, you guys," Billy said again. "Let's go."

They all went out of the big wooden door of the Crow's Nest. The rain had stopped at last and there was clear, pale-blue sky to the west.

Bobby and Chris got into Chris's car, and Alfred and his girlfriend got into their car. The rest of the crew walked to the boat.

Chris drove slowly to the *Andrea Gail* and stopped in front of her. Bobby looked at his girlfriend.

"I really don't want to go on this trip," he said suddenly. "I really don't want to go."

Chris put her arms around him and held him tightly.

"Well, don't go, then," she said quietly. "Please don't go, Bobby."

"I have to go, you know that," replied Bobby. "I need the money."

Billy Tyne walked over to the car and leaned in through the window. He, too, felt sorry for Bobby and Chris.

"Are you two going to be OK?" he asked.

Chris nodded her head. Bobby was almost crying. He turned his head away so that Billy couldn't see his face.

"All right, then," said Billy. "Goodbye, Chris. We'll see you when we get back."

Billy walked back to the *Andrea Gail* and jumped down onto the deck of the boat. Then Sully came over to Chris's car. He had known Bobby for most of his life, and he was worried about the young man. Was Bobby making a huge mistake?

"Are you two really OK?" he asked Bobby and Chris. "Are you *sure* that you're OK?"

"Yes, we're OK," replied Chris. "Please give us one more minute."

Sully smiled and walked away. Bugsy and Murph didn't have anybody to say goodbye to, so they got onto the boat quickly. Then Alfred got out of his car and walked across to the *Andrea Gail*. His girlfriend stayed in the car, crying. She looked at Chris and moved two fingers down her cheeks. "Yes, I'm sad too," she was saying.

Now there were five men on the boat, waiting for Bobby.

"I've got to go," he said quietly.

"Yes," replied Chris.

"Remember this, Christina," Bobby said, looking into her eyes. "Remember that I'll always love you. Please remember!"

Chris smiled at him, as the tears ran down her face.

"Yes, I know," she whispered.

Bobby kissed her, then got out of the car, still holding her hand. He let go of her hand, closed the car door, and gave her a last smile. Then he walked across to the *Andrea Gail*. He didn't look back.

4

The Grand Banks

The *Andrea Gail* was a large and powerful swordfishing boat. She had been built in Panama City, Florida, in 1978. She was 72 feet long and her hull was made of strong steel plates[31]. Her engine had a strength of 356 horsepower[32] and she could travel at a speed of 12 knots[33].

In 1987, some changes had been made to the *Andrea Gail*, and some extra equipment had been added to her. The back of the boat—her stern—was extended. It was made longer by three feet, so that two extra fuel tanks could be fixed there. The *Andrea Gail* could carry 1,900 gallons of fuel in each of these tanks.

The whaleback deck was also extended. Now, more than 30 drums of fuel or water, and the ice machine, could be stored there. In total, about ten extra tons of fuel, steel, and machinery were added to the *Andrea Gail*. So the boat was now carrying a lot of extra weight. She was much heavier than before. When she was at sea, more of her hull would be under the water. If a large wave knocked her onto her side, she would take much longer to roll upright again.

But the *Andrea Gail* could now carry enough fuel, and make enough ice, to stay out at sea for six weeks. She did not have to come back to port during that time. So she could catch more fish and make more money on each trip. And every person who ever fished with her was interested in making money. So none of them disagreed with the changes that were made.

The *Andrea Gail* was a good, strong boat. She had been

inspected[34] in November 1990 by a company called Marine Safety Consultants. This company sent inspectors to check boats. The inspectors made sure that the boats were safe to go out to sea. The inspector who checked the *Andrea Gail* wrote a report. In his report he said, "This boat is well suited for its purpose." He thought that the boat was well built for the work that she had to do. He couldn't find anything seriously wrong with her.

The *Andrea Gail* had all the correct equipment to cope with[35] problems at sea. There were six survival suits on board—one for each member of the crew. These suits were made of a special kind of material that wouldn't sink. So if a man wearing a survival suit fell into the sea, the suit would keep him on the surface of the water.

The Andrea Gail also had a life raft. If the fishing boat was damaged and began to sink, the crew could inflate this small rubber boat. When it was filled with air, the crew could climb into the life raft and float in it until a ship or helicopter came to rescue them.

———

The Grand Banks are very good fishing grounds with plenty of fish, but they are also one of the worst areas in the world for storms.

The Grand Banks are about 1,200 miles northeast of Gloucester and about 400 miles south of Newfoundland, which is part of Canada. Most of the Grand Banks are in Canadian national waters[36], so U.S. boats are not allowed to fish there. But two areas of the Grand Banks are *outside* Canadian national waters. These are called the "Nose" and the "Tail" of the Banks.

When the *Andrea Gail* left Gloucester on the afternoon of

September 20th, she was heading for the Tail of the Banks. She took about a week to get there. The crew passed the time by repairing their fishing equipment, sleeping, watching videos, and reading. Every evening, at about eight o'clock, the men had dinner together. They sat around the table in the galley, talking about normal things—work, women, children, and sports. They also talked a lot about fishing. Murph was the ship's cook and he always prepared the dinner.

The men took turns at being on watch. For two hours, twice a day, each man sat in the pilothouse of the boat, looking out to sea. The pilothouse of a boat is where the helm, radar, and navigational instruments[37] are. The man on watch checked these instruments from time to time. He made sure that the boat was in no danger. But he didn't have to touch the helm—he didn't have to steer the boat. Billy Tyne set the *Andrea Gail*'s course[38] and she was steered automatically by the autopilot[39]. Most of the time, the man on watch sat and stared at the sea. The shapes and colors of the waves were always interesting to look at.

Captain Billy Tyne was different from most fishermen. Most fishermen go to sea because they need the money, but Billy fished because he really loved the job. He'd been out to the Grand Banks many times and he'd fished in lots of other places too—the Carolinas, Florida, and the Caribbean Islands.

Billy was a very skillful and experienced fisherman. He was also a very lucky one because he always knew where to find fish. Billy's marriage had ended because he was away from home so much. His ex-wife, Jodi, had complained that fishing was more important to Billy then she was, and she had been right. But she understood Billy's skill and his luck.

"It's a strange thing," Jodi used to say. "It's as if Billy has a kind of radar inside his head. He always knows where to find fish. Not many fishermen can go out and catch fish all the time, but Billy can. Everyone wants to go on a fishing trip with Billy because he always makes a lot of money."

On September 27th, the *Andrea Gail* reached the Tail of the Banks and the crew began to fish. For the first week, the wind was blowing from the northwest and the sky was a deep blue color. It was hot during the day and the men wore T-shirts on deck. In the evenings, when it was cool, they wore jackets and sweatshirts as they fastened the fish bait to the gangions. They finished work every evening at about ten o'clock. Then everyone except the man on watch went to their bunks[40] to sleep for a few hours. In the early morning they all woke and began hauling the mainline in.

When the *Andrea Gail* first arrived at the Tail, Billy Tyne saw another swordfishing boat a few miles away. This boat was the *Mary T*, whose home port was Fairhaven, a fishing town which is south of Gloucester. Her captain was a man from Florida, named Albert Johnston. The *Mary T* had come out to the Tail before Billy's boat.

The two boats fished only a few miles apart for about a week. Then on October 5th, Albert Johnston sent a radio message to Billy.

"I'm heading back to port," Albert said. "I'll let you know about the weather as I go."

The weather systems[41] off the east coast of North America usually move from west to east. Albert Johnston was heading west, back towards the shore, so he would pass through each weather system before it reached Billy. He would be able to tell Billy what kind of weather was on its way towards him.

41

Albert headed back to port. He had been at sea for more than a month. He reached Fairhaven on October 12th and unloaded his catch there. But he didn't plan to stay in port for very long. He needed to make a few repairs to his boat. After that, he wanted to go out on another trip before the bad weather started. It was getting very late in the year to go to the Grand Banks, and every day the danger of storms was greater.

"The longer we wait, the worse the storms will be," Albert told his crew. "If we get into bad weather on the Grand Banks, we'll be in really big trouble."

But the first bad weather came when Albert's boat was still in the harbor in Fairhaven. And soon after the bad weather arrived in Fairhaven, it caught the *Andrea Gail* out at the Grand Banks.

It was morning, and the men were working on the deck, hauling the fish into the boat. Suddenly the wind began to blow hard[42] and the waves started coming over the deck. Soon the wind was blowing at a speed of 30 knots. But the men couldn't stop working and go below deck until they had hauled in all the fish.

Suddenly, the *Andrea Gail's* crew saw an enormous wave rising up above them. It was about 30 feet high. The crew saw the white line of foam[43] at its top. But they didn't have time to see much more. The wave crashed down on the deck of the *Andrea Gail* and covered her with tons of water.

The *Andrea Gail* was knocked over onto her side by the wave. Then very slowly, she rolled upright again. Billy Tyne sent a radio message to the other boats in the area to tell them what had happened.

"We've just been hit by a 30-foot wave," Billy said. "The boat was over on her side. For a moment, I thought that the

The wave crashed down on the deck of the Andrea Gail and covered her with tons of water.

Andrea Gail was going to turn upside-down."

When Albert Johnston heard Billy's news about the huge wave, he was surprised and worried.

"The *Andrea Gail* is a good, strong boat," he thought. "But Billy said that the big wave nearly rolled her upside-down. Why was that? A boat like the *Andrea Gail* shouldn't roll over so easily. Something must be wrong with her."

———

The weather got better again and Billy Tyne kept the *Andrea Gail* at the Tail of the Banks for another week. But the trip wasn't going well. Billy's luck had disappeared. His men weren't catching enough fish. They were using up all their fish bait, and they'd eaten a lot of their own food.

"We've got to find more fish soon," thought Billy.

That evening, after dinner, he talked to the five other crew members.

"Listen, guys," he said, "we've got a problem. We're not doing very well here. If we don't start catching more fish, we'll only make enough money to cover the expenses of the trip. We'll only have earned enough to pay for our food and equipment. There won't be enough to pay us as well."

"What do you suggest, Billy?" asked Bobby. "What shall we do? We're not going to go home now, are we?"

"No," replied Billy slowly. "I have an idea, but maybe you won't agree with me. We *could* go to the Flemish Cap."

The men stared at Billy.

"But the Flemish Cap is a very long way from here," said Murph, after a moment. "It's right at the edge of the fishing charts[44]. And out there, the weather can be very risky—very dangerous. It's even worse than at the Grand Banks. You can get terrible storms at the Flemish Cap at this time of year."

"Yes, I know that," said Billy. "But that's where the fish are, I'm sure of it. It's nearly the end of the fishing season and this trip is our last chance of making money for the year. Now, do you want to make some money, or don't you?"

Each man in the crew was thinking carefully. If the *Andrea Gail* got into trouble at the Flemish Cap, it would be difficult for anybody to rescue them. But Billy thought that there were plenty of fish at the Cap, and Billy wasn't often wrong about fish. If he was right this time, they would all be able to make a lot of money. And that was the only reason that they had come on the trip.

Going to the Flemish Cap was dangerous, but they had no choice. If they wanted to finish this job, earn some money, and get home quickly, they had to go to the Cap. They all agreed about that.

"All right, Billy," one of them said at last. "We agree with you. Let's go to the Flemish Cap."

5

First Warnings

The Flemish Cap was a long way from where the *Andrea Gail* was fishing. Billy Tyne would need more fuel to get there, and return to port. He had an idea.

The owner of the *Andrea Gail*, Bob Brown, also owned a swordfishing boat called the *Hannah Boden*. The captain of the *Hannah Boden* was a woman named Linda Greenlaw. Like Billy Tyne, she was one of the best swordfishing captains who worked off the east coast of North America. The *Andrea Gail* and the *Hannah Boden* caught a lot of fish and made a lot of money for Bob Brown.

After the *Andrea Gail* had left Gloucester on September 20th, several other Gloucester boats had come out to the Grand Banks too.

The *Hannah Boden* was one of these boats. She was fishing further east than Billy, at a place which was directly south of the Flemish Cap. The *Andrea Gail* would pass close to her on the way to the Cap.

The *Andrea Gail* and the *Hannah Boden* often helped each other at sea. So now Billy Tyne called Linda Greenlaw on his radio.

"Hi, Linda," he said. "I've got a problem. I'm heading for the Flemish Cap, but I haven't got enough fuel. Can you help me?"

"The Flemish Cap?" asked Linda in surprise. "That's a very long way, Billy. I've got plenty of fuel and you can certainly have some. But why are you going all the way to the Flemish Cap? It's late in the season now and it's risky to go there."

"I know that," replied Billy. "But we couldn't find enough

fish at the Tail. And there are plenty of fish at the Flemish Cap."

"OK, Billy," said Linda. "Of course I'll help you. But please be careful."

Linda told Billy the position of the *Hannah Boden*. Billy set the *Andrea Gail*'s course and, later that day, he brought her up behind the *Hannah Boden* in the ocean. Now the stern of the *Hannah Boden* was directly ahead of the bow of the *Andrea Gail*. The crews tied the boats together with ropes and pumped[45] fuel from the *Hannah Boden*'s tanks into the tanks of the *Andrea Gail*.

Later, the two boats separated and the crews waved goodbye to each other. The *Andrea Gail* headed off north in the direction of the Flemish Cap.

In half an hour, the crew of the *Hannah Boden* could no longer see the *Andrea Gail* on the ocean. She was only a small square on the *Hannah Boden*'s radar screen.

Linda Greenlaw watched the dot on the screen. She was worried.

"I hope that Billy knows what he's doing," she thought.

Billy Tyne now had enough fuel for the trip to the Flemish Cap, but he had other problems. The ice machine was no longer working properly. It should have been making three tons of ice every day. But something had gone wrong with the machine, and it was only making about one ton.

This was a serious problem for the *Andrea Gail*. If there wasn't enough ice to keep the fish that were caught each day fresh, the fish would start to lose their quality. People wouldn't pay high prices for fish that weren't fresh. So Billy would have to stay out at the fishing grounds for longer. And each day, he could only catch the amount of fish that he could freeze with one ton of ice.

But if the *Andrea Gail* stayed out at sea for too long, there would be another problem. Six men can't easily stay together on a small boat for a long time. They get angry with each other and they start fighting. Billy was an excellent captain and his crew were all friends. But even good friends can start behaving in a crazy way if they are at sea together for too long.

"We've got to find more fish," thought Billy. "Then we must get them back to Gloucester as quickly as possible. We've been at sea for three weeks already. We mustn't stay out for more than another two weeks."

During the fishing trip, Billy hadn't called Bob Brown, the owner of the *Andrea Gail*, on the radio. Billy didn't like speaking to Bob Brown.

Bob Brown owned five swordfishing boats whose home port was Gloucester. He made hundreds of thousands of dollars every year. He was a very strong and tough man who had worked hard all his life. And in the past he had gone on some very dangerous trips. In those days, he usually sailed alone because nobody wanted to go with him. He wasn't very popular.

Bob Brown was a successful businessman, but he was still not very popular with the people of Gloucester. He had a bad reputation. In 1980, a man was lost from one of Bob's boats—a boat called *Sea Fever*. This man was swept over the side of the boat during a bad storm. Bob Brown was not on board the *Sea Fever* at the time, and the man's death was not his fault. But after that, some people started calling the owner,

"Suicide Brown." They meant, "If you work for him, your life is in danger."

The same thing happened again a few years later, in the mid-1980s. This time Bob Brown was out on the Grand Banks himself, on the *Hannah Boden*. A huge wave hit the boat and two men were swept overboard. One of them was rescued, but the other man sank and drowned quickly. And after that, more people began to think that it was unlucky to go on a trip with one of Bob Brown's boats. So maybe this was why—like most people from Gloucester—Billy Tyne never spoke to Bob Brown if he didn't have to speak to him. And now, he didn't call Bob to tell him about his change of plan.

———

After the *Andrea Gail* reached the Flemish Cap, Billy Tyne's luck started to change. He had been right—there were plenty of fish at the Flemish Cap. Soon the crew was catching between 5,000 and 6,000 pounds of swordfish every day. By the end of the month, they had 40,000 pounds of fish in the fish hold. The catch was worth about $160,000.

On October 24th, Billy Tyne called Albert Johnston, the captain of the *Mary T*, on his radio. Billy's voice sounded very happy.

"We're hauling in our fishing gear[46] and then we'll head for home," he said. "We've got enough fish in our hold now. We have to get back to port fast."

Billy had a huge amount of swordfish in his hold. But he still had problems with the ice machine, so he couldn't keep the fish fresh for much longer. He had to get back to Gloucester as quickly as possible. The other Gloucester swordfishing boats had left the port later than Billy and they were still fishing. So if Billy got back to Gloucester quickly,

Soon the crew was catching between 5,000 and 6,000 pounds of swordfish every day.

the *Andrea Gail* would be the only boat in the port. Her catch could be sold at the best price.

On October 25th, the *Andrea Gail* started her long journey to Gloucester. It would take her about a week to return to port. But Billy and the crew were happy now. If they could get home in a week, there would be enough ice to keep all the fish fresh. It had been a very good trip. The weather was clear and the sky was blue. Everything seemed perfect.

But about 2,000 miles away, unusual things were happening to the weather—unusual and very, very dangerous things.

————

Fishing boat captains listen to weather forecasts a lot when they are fishing. But they don't listen to them so often when they are heading for home. At the end of a fishing trip, captains haul their fishing gear out of the water and head straight back to port. They want to get home as quickly as possible. That was what Billy wanted to do now, but there *was* something else that he had to think about. He had to think about Sable Island.

Sable Island lies southeast of Nova Scotia. The sea around the island is very dangerous, and there is often bad weather around Sable Island too. Many boats have sunk there. Billy didn't want to go too near to Sable Island. He set the *Andrea Gail*'s course so that she would pass the island many miles to the south.

Two-and-a-half days after leaving the Flemish Cap, the *Andrea Gail* had traveled about 450 miles and the weather was still calm. At 3:15 p.m. on the afternoon of October 27th, Billy called the Canadian Coast Guard[47] to tell them that he was entering Canadian national waters.

"This is the U.S. fishing boat *Andrea Gail*," Billy said.

"Our position is 44:25 degrees north, 49:05 degrees west[48], and we're heading for Gloucester, Massachusetts."

"That's fine," replied the Coast Guard, "Go ahead."

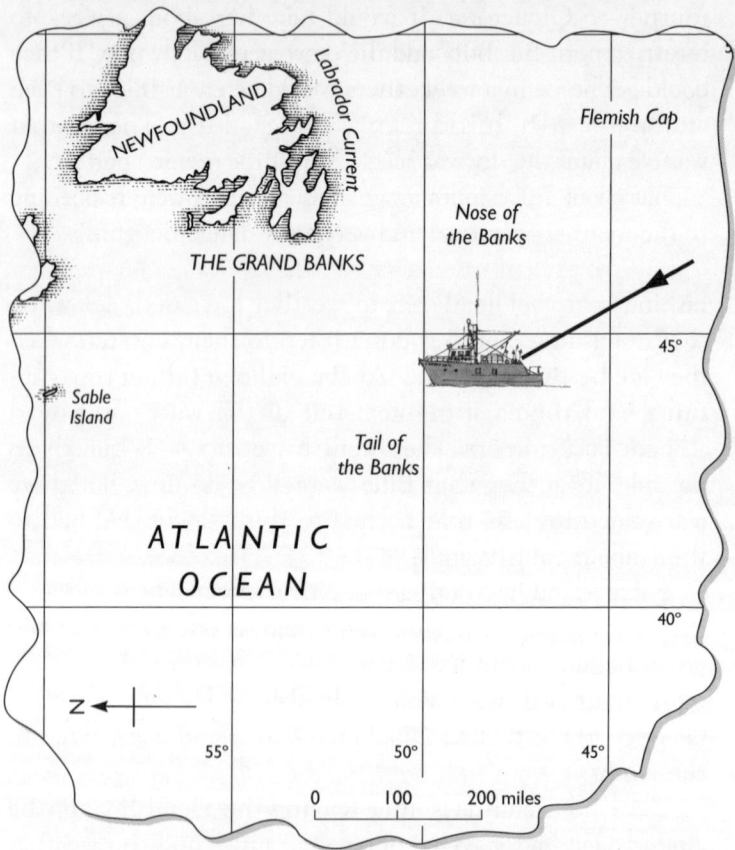

All the other fishing boats in the New England swordfishing fleet were a long way from the *Andrea Gail*. Most of them were fishing about 200 miles to the east of Billy's position. Albert Johnston on the *Mary T* was about 200 miles to the south. But Billy had already finished his trip and was heading west, away from the other boats and straight towards Gloucester and home.

———

That evening, the Canadian Weather Service sent all the fishing boats a fax of a weather chart[49]—a map showing the weather off the Canadian coast. The chart was very unusual because it showed three completely different weather systems, and each one was heading straight for the Grand Banks.

There was a hurricane, called Hurricane "Grace," moving towards the north from near the island of Bermuda. There was a front of cold air[50] moving towards the south, from the north of Canada. And there was a storm moving east from the Great Lakes in North America. This storm was traveling straight towards Sable Island.

A few minutes after she received the fax, Linda Greenlaw, the captain of the *Hannah Boden*, called Billy on her radio. Her voice sounded worried.

"Hey, Billy," she said, "have you seen the new weather chart?"

"Yes," replied Billy. "I've seen it."

"What do you think?" Linda asked.

"It looks as if we're going to have some rough weather," Billy said. Then he and Linda talked for a few more minutes. They arranged to talk again the next day and they said goodbye. Afterwards, Billy went down to the galley, to eat dinner with the rest of the crew.

Linda felt very worried about Billy. The *Hannah Boden* was about 500 hundred miles east of the *Andrea Gail*. The bad weather was coming from the west, so it would hit the *Andrea Gail* first.

"Billy is heading directly into the bad weather," thought Linda.

But Billy felt quite happy. A boat like the *Andrea Gail* wouldn't sink easily. She had a steel hull, and she had 40,000 pounds of fish in her hold. All this extra weight meant that much more of her hull was under the water than when she was empty. For this reason she was even more stable than usual—she wouldn't roll over easily, even in big waves. But if she did roll over, she would roll back very slowly.

The air was calm that evening. The sky was clear and full of stars and there was a half-moon. A light wind was blowing from the northwest. The sea was peaceful and beautiful in the moonlight.

"Everything will be all right," thought Billy. "We'll soon be home."

———

During the night, the *Andrea Gail* passed to the north of the *Mary T*. By dawn on the morning of October 28th, the *Andrea Gail* was almost at the edge of the Grand Banks and she was nearly halfway home.

But just after dawn, something strange happened to the weather. The wind started to change direction. Finally the wind was blowing from the southeast, not the northwest. And then the *Andrea Gail* received another weather fax.

6

Into the Storm

Every boat in the swordfishing fleet received the fax of the weather chart from the Canadian Weather Service. Each captain then had to decide what was the best thing to do for his boat and his crew.

Albert Johnston, the captain of the *Mary T*, decided to head northwest into an area of colder water. Cold water is heavier than warm water, and Albert thought that the waves would not get so big where the water was cold. The rest of the swordfishing fleet, including the *Hannah Boden*, stayed far to the east and waited to see what the storm was going to do.

But the *Andrea Gail* kept on going west, heading straight into the bad weather, right into the path[51] of the storm.

Why did Billy Tyne decide not to change the *Andrea Gail*'s course? Why didn't he try to get out of the path of the storm? Was it because he had a hold full of fish and not enough ice to stay at sea any longer? Was it because he'd been at sea for more than a month, and he just wanted to get home as fast as possible? No one will ever know.

Billy had been a fisherman for many years and he'd been in many bad storms before. He was also a very experienced captain. When the weather chart came out of the fax machine, he must have known at once that it was a serious warning. He must have known that the *Andrea Gail* was heading into a dangerous storm. He must have told the crew to prepare for bad weather.

The crew of a boat has to do several things to get it ready for a storm. First, they have to close all the doors and windows, to stop the sea from pouring into the boat. They have to take all their fishing gear off the deck, and tie the fuel and water drums to the deck so that nothing can come loose in the strong winds.

Then the captain has to go to the engine room[52] and check everything there. He has to make sure that the fire alarm and the high-water alarm[53] are turned on and that the pumps are working. If seawater comes pouring into the engine room, the crew has to be able to pump the water out before it damages the engine. The emergency lighting[54] has to be checked, and the crew's survival suits have to be checked.

When all this has been done, the captain and the crew have to sit and wait for the storm to hit the boat.

———

The headquarters of the U.S. National Weather Service[55] is in Boston, on the first floor of a building at Logan Airport. On October 28th, 1991, several meteorologists were working there. Most of them were sitting in front of their computer screens, staring at information from satellite photos[56]. Bob Case, the chief meteorologist in the room, was walking up and down between the desks. In the last two days, he had seen some very interesting and unusual things on the weather charts.

The satellite photos showed a front of cold air moving south from Canada. They also showed a line of clear dry air like a small wave. This line of clear dry air was moving east from the Great Lakes and was the beginning of a storm. It was moving in the direction of Sable Island. At the same time, Hurricane Grace was moving north up the U.S. coast. It was heading towards the area of the Grand Banks.

Bob Case was a very experienced meteorologist, but he had never seen anything quite like this before. He knew that weather systems only came together like this maybe once in a hundred years. Case knew that something incredible and terrible was going to happen.

"Hurricane Grace is going to hit the cold front," thought Bob Case. "Hurricanes contain warm, light air and the cold front is like a wall of *cold air*. So Hurricane Grace will bounce off [57] the cold front like a rubber ball. And it will bounce straight into the path of the storm which is heading for Sable Island.

"Three powerful weather systems are heading towards each other and they're going to collide. They're going to hit each other. The result will be like a huge bomb exploding out at sea. There will be a storm more terrible than anyone can imagine. It will be the perfect storm!"

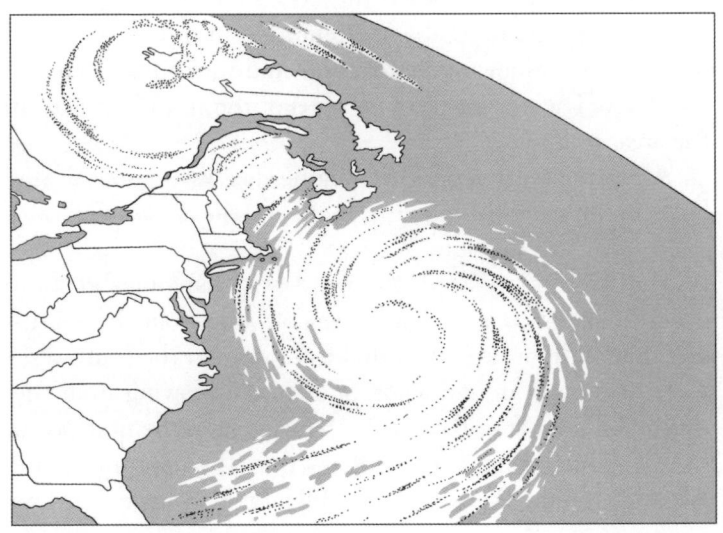

The storm from the Great Lakes was still small, but it was getting stronger all the time. It traveled southeast across Nova Scotia. By dawn on Monday October 28th, it was just north of Sable Island, and about two hundred miles from the *Andrea Gail*.

———

The Canadian government had nine data buoys in the water off the coast of North America between Boston and the Grand Banks. Data buoys record information about the weather out at sea—the height of the waves and the speed of the wind. The buoys transmit this information to the shore every hour, using radio signals.

One of these data buoys—its number was 44139—was about 70 miles east of Sable Island, very near to the position of the *Andrea Gail* on the morning of Monday, October 28th. All morning the sea had been calm. And on the shore, the instruments which recorded the buoy's data were steady all morning. But then, at about 2 p.m., the instruments started to show winds blowing at 15 knots and waves that were 12 feet high. These were the first signs of the storm's arrival in the area.

A few hours later, another weather fax was sent to all the boats in the swordfishing fleet, including the *Andrea Gail*.

———

As the afternoon passed, the wind was changing direction every hour. At four o'clock it was blowing from the southeast, but an hour later it started to blow from the southwest. Then it moved around again and started blowing from the north. An hour after that, it was blowing from the northwest.

At about 6 p.m. on October 28th, the captain of the *Allison*—Tommy Barrie—called Billy Tyne on his radio. The

Allison was one of the other boats in the swordfishing fleet. Tommy's boat was about 600 miles east of the *Andrea Gail*. The captain of the *Allison* wanted to know if it would be safe to put his fishing gear into the water that night.

"What's the weather like where you are, Billy?" asked Tommy.

"I'm 130 miles east of Sable Island. The weather was calm earlier, but it's getting bad now," replied Billy. "The wind is blowing at 50 to 80 knots and the waves are 30 feet high. But I'm still heading for home."

"OK," said Tommy. "We won't put our fishing gear into the water tonight. Maybe the weather will get better later. Let's talk again in a few hours, at about eleven o'clock."

"OK, that's fine," said Billy. "I'll call you at eleven and tell you what's happening where I am then."

"Thanks, Billy," said Tommy. "I look forward to hearing from you."

After his conversation with Tommy Barrie, Billy sent a message to all the other boats in the swordfishing fleet.

"The weather is getting bad out here, guys," he said. "It's getting very bad."

That was the last time that anybody heard from Billy Tyne or the *Andrea Gail*.

———

Linda Greenlaw, the captain of the *Hannah Boden*, heard Billy's message and she was extremely worried.

"I'm afraid for Billy," she thought. "He sounded frightened and Billy doesn't get frightened. This storm is going to be really bad."

The storm must have first hit the *Andrea Gail* at just after 7 p.m. By then, the storm had enormous power and it was getting stronger and stronger all the time. By 8 p.m. the winds were blowing at 40 knots and the waves were doubling in size. The biggest waves were starting at 35 feet high, falling, then re-appearing at almost 70 feet high.

Soon the *Andrea Gail* must have been in serious trouble.

———

The center of the storm was close to Sable Island. But hundreds of miles to the west of Sable Island and the *Andrea Gail*, a different kind of boat was in danger from the same storm. This was a sailing yacht called the *Satori*.

The *Satori* belonged to a retired seaman named Ray Leonard. During the summer, Ray kept the *Satori* at Portsmouth, a town on the east coast of the U.S., north of Gloucester. But he now planned to sail the yacht to Bermuda for the winter months. He'd found two people to work as crew and help him on the trip. They were both women— Karen Stimpson and Sue Bylander.

Karen Stimpson was forty-two years old. She was a very experienced sailor who had crossed the Atlantic Ocean on boats many times. She had no husband or children—her great love was the sea. Sue Bylander was her friend.

Ray, Karen, and Sue left Portsmouth on the *Satori* during the last week in October.

They sailed down the Piscataqua River to the Atlantic Ocean. They were heading for the Great South Channel between Georges Bank and Cape Cod. From there, they were going to sail south to Bermuda.

On Saturday, October 26th, the weather was calm. The sky was blue and there was a light wind. It was perfect weather for sailing. It was so warm that Karen and Sue wore T-shirts on deck.

It was perfect weather for sailing.

Towards evening, the weather became misty[58]. By the time it got dark, the sea was strangely quiet, as if it was waiting for something to happen.

Karen, Sue, and Ray were having dinner in the cabin.

"You heard the weather forecast this evening, didn't you?" Karen asked Ray. "You heard that there was a cold front moving south?"

"Yes," replied Ray. "But it won't be a problem for us. If the weather gets bad, we don't have to worry. We can sail into Buzzard's Bay. We can shelter near the shore. The water is much calmer there. But I really don't want to go close to the shore. I prefer sailing out on the open ocean—it's much more exciting."

Ray Leonard was Karen and Sue's employer. He was paying them, so they had to do what he told them. They couldn't take the *Satori* nearer to the shore if he didn't want them to do that.

So the *Satori* sailed on. By the time she reached the end of the Great South Channel, the waves were getting larger and larger.

On the afternoon of Sunday, October 27th, the crew heard another weather forecast on their radio.

———

Karen was an experienced sailor, but she was starting to feel afraid. All night, the weather kept getting worse and worse. By dawn on Monday, October 28th, the waves were huge and the wind was very strong. The sea was an unpleasant gray color.

Karen tried talking to Ray again about the danger they were in. But he wouldn't listen to her.

"There's going to be a really bad storm," Karen said. "I think that we should change our course while we can, before it's too late."

"Don't worry," replied Ray. "Everything will be fine. The wind will lose its strength in twenty-four hours. It will soon be calm again."

"I don't think so," said Karen. "I've got a bad feeling about this storm."

On the evening of Monday, October 28th, Karen, Sue, and Ray ate dinner in the cabin of the *Satori*. They were spending as much time as possible there, because it was so cold and wet up on the deck.

"We can't go into the shore now," said Ray. "It's too dangerous. We would have to cross the shipping lanes[59] and large ships could collide with us. But we're quite safe here."

But it was getting more and more difficult for the *Satori* to keep moving forward. She was only a 32-foot sailing yacht, not a large fishing boat.

The wind was now blowing at 50 knots and the waves were rising up like huge dark mountains. Karen and Sue tied themselves to the *Satori* with safety lines[60]. They took turns at the helm, trying to steer a course through the waves.

The storm was the worst that Karen had ever seen and she was very, very frightened.

"We're going to die," she thought. "We're all going to die!"

7

What Happened to the Andrea Gail?

Meanwhile, what had happened to the *Andrea Gail?* When Billy Tyne had spoken to Tommy Barrie on the radio at about 6 p.m. on Monday, October 28th, he'd said that he would call Tommy again at 11 p.m. Billy had said that he would give Tommy another report on the weather in his area.

At 11 p.m. the captain of the *Allison* waited for Billy's call, but it never came. Was Billy busy in the storm, or had he just forgotten to call? At about midnight, Tommy tried to call Billy but he couldn't get through to the *Andrea Gail's* radio. This was a serious situation[61] and Tommy was worried.

"Perhaps the *Andrea Gail* has lost her radio antennas[62] in the storm," he thought.

Without radio antennas, a boat cannot communicate with other boats, or with the shore. The antennas on the *Andrea Gail* were fixed high up on a steel mast behind the pilot-house. But the antennas were not very strong, and a really large wave could easily knock them down.

If the *Andrea Gail* had lost her antennas, she would no longer have been able to communicate with other boats. Billy wouldn't have been able to contact the Coast Guard. He would no longer have been able to send or receive faxes. Also, part of the boat's navigational system would have been destroyed and Billy wouldn't have known exactly where he was.

If a big wave had destroyed the antennas, maybe it had also destroyed the *Andrea Gail's* radar. Then Billy wouldn't have known what other boats were in the area. For Billy, it would have been like sailing in the nineteenth century.

What did happen to the *Andrea Gail?* We will never know. But there are some things that we do know. At around midnight, the data buoy nearest to Sable Island recorded that the windspeed lessened and the waves became a little smaller. The waves were then about 45 feet high, the same as the *Andrea Gail's* length. At that point, the fishing boat must have been climbing slowly up each wave, then going over the top and falling down the other side.

But an hour later, the waves had got higher again and the winds had got stronger. Some waves were about 100 feet high. Billy Tyne had been in many storms but he could never have seen anything like that before. Few people have seen waves like that and lived to tell about them.

The center of the storm was now over Sable Island. Sable Island is like a bar of sand about 70 miles long. But only about 20 miles of this long, sandy island are above the surface of the ocean. The other 50 miles of sand are just below the surface. The water which covers the sand bar is shallow, but it is also very dangerous. There are strong currents[63] over the hidden sand. So a boat can easily get pulled into the shallow water by the currents. There, it can be smashed to pieces by the waves.

Some people say that 5,000 men have drowned in the shallow water at Sable Island. So the island has a sad and terrible history. People call Sable Island, "The Graveyard of the Atlantic." But the bodies of many people who have drowned there have never been found.

In the days before radar and radio navigational systems, many ships sank off Sable Island because their captains made mistakes in navigation. If Billy lost his radio antennas and his radar stopped working, he probably made the same mistakes as those men.

———

The moon was covered with clouds that night, and huge waves like mountains must have been all around the boat. All the time, the winds must have been pushing the *Andrea Gail* further and further west, right into the dangerous shallow water around Sable Island.

The *Andrea Gail* didn't have a chance to escape. At about midnight, something terrible must have happened to her.

But one thing is very strange. No distress signal[64] was ever received from the *Andrea Gail's* EPIRB[65]. Each EPIRB has a different number, and the number of the *Andrea Gail's* EPIRB was 986. But the Canadian Coast Guard has said that it received no signal from EPIRB 986 on the night of October 28th.

It is *not* strange that Billy Tyne didn't call the Coast Guard on his radio on the night of October 28th. If the *Andrea Gail's* antennas had been lost in the storm, Billy couldn't have sent a radio message. But EPIRB works in a different way—it doesn't need the antennas. All Billy had to do was to switch on the machine.

———

Did the six men on the *Andrea Gail*—Billy, Bobby, Bugsy, Alfred, Sully, and Murph—know that they were going to die that night?

Billy, up in the pilothouse, trying to steer the boat through the waves, probably had no time to feel afraid. The five other men were probably in the galley, thinking about their girlfriends and their families. They couldn't do anything else. They could only wait to die. Rescue was almost impossible in that terrible storm. The life raft was useless—a raft would quickly sink in those huge waves. When the sea water started to pour into the *Andrea Gail*, and she started to sink, all of the men must have known that it was the end.

The most experienced men on the *Andrea Gail* were Billy, Bugsy, and Murph. They had been on many trips together. At home, Billy had a photo of the three of them with a huge swordfish. In the picture, they were holding the fish and laughing.

Murph had had some very strange experiences at sea, but he'd always been lucky. He'd been in some bad accidents and had nearly died several times. One time, a shark had gotten his arm in its mouth. Murph's friends beat the shark to death[66], and Murph was taken to a hospital by helicopter.

Another time, his hand was caught on a hook and he was dragged off his boat, down into the sea. He was pulled along by the fishing line for a long way. Fortunately, another fisherman had seen the accident, and he was able to pull Murph back into the boat.

"I thought that I was going to die," Murph had said later.

The worst accident happened one hot night. Murph had tried to sleep in his bunk but he was too warm, so he went up onto the deck. A few minutes later, a British submarine[67] collided with the boat. The submarine made a huge hole in the fishing boat's hull and it destroyed Murph's bunk. He was very lucky that night.

When Murph had first met his wife, Debra, he'd told her that he would die before he was thirty years old. But she married him anyway and they had a little boy. Later, the marriage ended, because Murph was never at home.

Before his last trip on the *Andrea Gail*, Murph did something strange. He went to see his mother and told her that he was going to die at sea.

"Do you still have all the prizes and awards I won at school?" he asked.

"Yes, of course I do," his mother replied in surprise.

"Please give them to my son when I'm dead."

After that, Murph left the house quickly. His mother watched him go. The strange conversation had made her feel surprised and afraid.

A few days later, Murph left Gloucester on the *Andrea Gail*. Did he guess that he would never return?

———

We cannot know for sure what it was like during those terrible last hours on the *Andrea Gail*. But we do know what it was like for other boats, out there in that dreadful storm.

The *Mary T* got hit by the storm a few hours after the *Andrea Gail*. When he received the first storm warning from the weather station, Albert Johnston, her captain, had decided to head north. He headed towards the Tail of the Grand Banks. He hoped that the weather conditions there would be safer for his boat. Later, he told people about the problems that the storm had made for him. He told them about the 100-knot winds and the 30-foot waves. He told them about the dreadful hour when Hurricane Grace and the storm from the west collided.

8

Rescuers in the Storm

Hurricane Grace was moving up the coast very fast. At about 8 a.m. on Tuesday, October 29th, it collided with the cold front moving down from Canada. When it hit the thick, cold air, the hurricane bounced off it like a ball, straight back out to sea. The hurricane was now traveling at about 80 knots, and it made 30-foot waves in the sea.

And that evening, at about 8 p.m., Hurricane Grace collided with the Sable Island storm. The result of this collision was so violent—like a huge bomb exploding—that Hurricane Grace began to break up.

Now the Sable Island storm was caught between the Canadian cold front and Hurricane Grace. Both the cold front and the breaking hurricane were spinning around very fast. As they spun, they pushed the storm back towards the west. So now the storm was traveling back towards the coast.

Most of the boats in the swordfishing fleet were about 500 miles to the east of Sable Island. Those boats escaped the worst part of the storm.

But the yacht *Satori* was in great danger. She was alone at the north end of the Great South Channel, between Georges Bank and Cape Cod. The terrible storm was now moving fast towards the west, and the *Satori* was right in its path.

On the *Satori*, Karen Stimpson had listened unhappily to the weather forecast on the morning of Tuesday, October 29th. She was very frightened.

Ray Leonard had said that the storm would get better, but he had been wrong. In fact, all day it had been getting worse.

The *Satori* was only a sailing yacht and she couldn't survive the huge waves and the terrible winds for very long. Karen knew this. Every time one of the huge waves hit her, the boat rolled onto her side.

Ray was lying on his bunk, not saying very much. Sue Bylander was in the cabin. She refused to go up on deck. So Karen put on all her warm clothes and went up on deck alone. The sails had already been taken down. But Karen tried to steer the boat through the waves. Soon she knew that she couldn't control the *Satori* any longer. The winds were too strong and the waves were too high.

The *Satori* was a sailing yacht, but she had an engine too. Karen thought about the engine. Then she went down the companionway[68] to talk to Ray.

"I can't steer the yacht any longer," she said. "She's out of control. We'll have to start her engine. Do you know how much fuel there is?"

Karen asked this question several times, but each time Ray gave a different answer.

"Either he doesn't know the answer, or he's crazy with fear," Karen told herself.

Suddenly, another huge wave caught the side of the *Satori*. The yacht rolled right over, so that her mast was in the water. Karen, Sue, and Ray were thrown against a wall, and the seawater poured down the companionway, into the cabin.

"Get a survival bag ready!" Karen shouted to Sue. "We have to abandon ship[69]. We have to get off the *Satori* fast, or we're all going to die!"

Sue grabbed a large bag and started filling it with clothes, food, and bottles of drinking water. Then she climbed up the companionway onto the deck, looking for the life raft. But the life raft had disappeared.

"Karen!" Sue screamed in terror. "The wind has blown the life raft away! It's gone! We can't get off the boat!"

Suddenly, Karen no longer felt afraid. There was no time for fear now. But she began to prepare for her death. The cabin was dark but she had a small flashlight. She sat down and wrote a few goodbye notes to her friends and family and put them in a small plastic bag. Sue was getting ready for death too. She came back into the cabin. She took her passport and stuck it onto her body with sticky tape. Now if anyone found her dead body, they would be able to identify her. They would know who she was.

"This is going to get worse," Karen thought. "But we're not going to die without a fight. We mustn't die on this boat."

Only Ray Leonard did nothing. He was still sitting on his bunk, staring in front of him.

"We have to send a Mayday call[70]!" Karen shouted to him.

The *Satori*'s radio was still working. Sue grabbed it and began to talk into it very fast. She said the same thing over and over again—

"This is the yacht, *Satori*. Our position is 39:49 degrees north and 69:52 degrees west. We are three people, this is a Mayday. If anyone can hear us, please give our position to the Coast Guard. I repeat, this is a Mayday message."

At 11:15 p.m., the captain of a larger boat heard Sue's terrified voice on his radio and he passed on her message to the U.S. Coast Guard. At once, the Coast Guard sent a Falcon jet plane out to find the *Satori*. The Coast Guard also sent a powerful ship—a cutter called the *Tamaroa*.

71

Sue was beginning to lose hope. She had repeated the Mayday message for half an hour and nobody had replied. She didn't know if anybody could hear her message. She didn't even know if there were other ships in the area.

Now Karen was up on deck. She was still trying to steer the yacht. The noise of the storm was very loud. But suddenly, she heard another sound—the sound of an airplane's engine. She looked up and saw the lights of the Falcon jet in the sky above her. A few minutes later, the Falcon's pilot called Sue on the radio and told her that the *Tamaroa* was on its way to rescue them.

"Karen, Karen!" shouted Sue excitedly. "We're going to be OK!"

Karen closed her eyes. She didn't feel excited, she felt calm and peaceful.

"I really thought that we were going to die tonight," she told herself. "But now we have a chance to live. We're going back to the world of living people."

The Falcon jet plane flew in circles around the *Satori*. The pilot kept telling Karen and Sue that everything would be OK.

"Don't worry," he said. "You're all alive. Soon you'll be safe and warm."

The *Tamaroa* was a powerful ship but she could only move slowly through the water. She wouldn't reach the *Satori* for another twelve hours. During this time, it was important that the *Satori* didn't sink. The yacht's crew had no survival suits. If they went into the sea, they would drown very quickly.

Ray Leonard was angry with Karen and Sue for sending the Mayday message. He was sure that the *Satori* was in no danger and he didn't want to be rescued.

"When the *Tamaroa* arrives, the captain will make me leave my boat," he thought. "But the *Satori* is my home, she's my life. If I leave her now, I'll probably never see her again. She'll sink to the bottom of the ocean. Well, I'm not going to leave her. Those two women can leave if they want, but I'm going to stay here."

———

All night, the *Tamaroa* moved slowly through the storm. Her commander, Lawrence Brudnicki, was hoping that he would reach the *Satori* before it was too late.

At dawn on the morning of Wednesday, October 30th, the U.S. Coast Guard sent a helicopter—an H-3—to replace the Falcon jet plane. This type of helicopter can only carry enough fuel for a few hours' flying, but it can drop a rescue basket into the sea on the end of a line. Then people can climb into the basket and the helicopter's crew can pull them up to safety.

The *Tamaroa* was still about five hours away from the *Satori's* position, and the storm was still getting worse. So the helicopter pilot, Claude Hessel, talked to Ray Leonard on his radio.

"We'll have to rescue you soon," Hessel said. "We can't wait much longer. If we don't take you off the boat soon, it will be too late."

"I don't *want* to be rescued," said Ray. "I'm not going to leave my boat."

This news was passed on to the *Tamaroa*. When Commander Brudnicki heard about it, he was angry. A plane, a helicopter, and a ship had all gone out in a dangerous storm to rescue Mr Leonard. Many people were risking their lives[71] to save him. And Mr Leonard was complaining that he didn't want to be rescued!

73

When the *Tamaroa* was only a few miles away from the *Satori*, Commander Brudnicki spoke to Ray Leonard on the radio himself.

"You have to get off your boat," he said angrily. "You don't have a choice. I'm ordering you to leave the boat."

An hour later, Commander Brudnicki and the crew of the *Tamaroa* could see the people on the *Satori*. Brudnicki decided that the best way to rescue the crew of the yacht was by dropping a raft into the water—a raft with an engine. Three members of the *Tamaroa*'s crew would take the raft to the *Satori*. Karen, Sue, and Ray could climb into the raft and be brought back to the *Tamaroa*.

At first everything went well. The raft reached the *Satori*, and the men in the raft threw survival suits to the yacht's crew. But then things started to go wrong. A huge wave pushed the *Satori* over, onto the raft. The yacht made a big hole in the raft. Water started to fill it and its engine stopped working. The rescuers were in trouble!

Now there were six people who needed to be rescued—Karen, Sue, Ray, and the three men from the *Tamaroa*'s raft.

Claude Hessel, the helicopter pilot, saw what had happened to the raft and called Commander Brudnicki on the radio.

"There's another way of doing this," the pilot said. "I can put a man into the water. He'll swim over to the yacht. Then I'll drop a rescue basket into the sea, and the swimmer can put the yacht's crew and your men into the basket, one by one. Then we can pull them up to the helicopter."

"OK, that will be fine," agreed Brudnicki. "There's nothing else we can do now. It's the best chance that they've got."

The rescue swimmer's name was Dave Moore and he was

twenty-five years old. He was very strong and healthy. Dave put on a neoprene wetsuit[72], socks, hood, and swimming fins on his feet. He pulled a mask and snorkel over his head. Finally he put on his neoprene gloves. He gave a sign that he was ready, and he sat down at the open door of the helicopter, waiting for the order to jump.

This was the first difficult rescue that Dave had taken part in. He looked down at the high waves and he felt the strong wind. But he wasn't nervous, he was only excited.

Meanwhile, Claude Hessel called the crew of the *Satori* on his radio.

"I'm putting a swimmer into the sea to rescue you," he told them. "We can't pick you up from your boat—it's too dangerous. We're going to pick you up from the water. Put on the survival suits and jump off the boat now. Stay together in a group and wait for the rescue swimmer."

Hessel saw Karen, Sue, and Ray put on the suits and jump into the sea. He gave the signal to Dave Moore to jump from the helicopter. Dave took a deep breath and jumped through the open door. He hit the water and started swimming towards the six people near the yacht. The noise of the wind was loud, but above the sound of the wind he could hear the helicopter. Its engine made a noise like thunder.

When Dave reached Karen, Sue, and Ray, he greeted them in a friendly way. He didn't want them to be worried or nervous.

"Hi, I'm Dave Moore, your rescue swimmer!" he shouted. "Who wants to go up first?"

Sue wanted to go first, so Dave grabbed the back of her survival suit and pulled her through the water. Claude Hessel had now dropped the rescue basket and Dave helped Sue climb into it. Twenty seconds later, she was safely in the helicopter and the basket was coming down again. Dave swam back for Karen and did the same thing for her. Then he went back for Ray Leonard. But Ray was much more difficult to rescue. He didn't try to help Dave at all. He lay like a dead man in the water. Dave had to pull him into the rescue basket.

After the crew of the *Satori* was safely in the helicopter, Dave rescued the three men from the *Tamaroa*'s raft in the same way. Finally he got into the basket himself and the helicopter pulled him up.

———

Claude Hessel flew the Coast Guard helicopter back to Cape Cod. When it landed, there were lots of TV and newspaper reporters waiting inside the Coast Guard station. They wanted to ask questions about the rescue. Everyone was very pleased and happy that the rescue had gone so well. They were very glad that Karen, Sue, and Ray were alive.

The only person who wasn't happy was Ray Leonard. He sat quietly on his own, not speaking.

"What's the matter with him?" asked one of the reporters. "Isn't he happy to be alive?"

"He didn't want to leave his boat," Karen explained. "The yacht was his home, and everything he owned was on it."

Leonard was unhappy, but he was a lucky man. Not everybody was as lucky as he was that night.

Above the sound of the wind, the helicopter's engine made a noise like thunder.

9

A Long Night for the Tamaroa

The Coast Guard cutter, the *Tamaroa*, was called to another rescue that night.

A National Guard[73] helicopter, an H-60, had been looking for a boat far out at sea. It was returning to the shore when it had run out of fuel. The helicopter had crashed into the ocean and had sunk immediately. There were five National Guardsmen on board, and they jumped out before the helicopter hit the water.

Now four of the men were together in the water, in a group. But none of them had seen the fifth man, after he jumped. The four men who stayed together were Dave Ruvola, Graham Buschor, Jim Mioli, and John Spillane. Dave and Graham were the pilots of the big helicopter and Jim was their engineer. John Spillane and the missing man—who was named Rick Smith—were rescue swimmers.

The Coast Guard headquarters at Boston knew exactly where the helicopter had crashed. So a Falcon jet plane, a helicopter—another H-3—and the *Tamaroa* were sent to find the men and rescue them.

The Falcon arrived at the position of the crash first. The pilot could see small lights in the water. The men in the water were carrying strobes—flashing lights—and these were the lights that the pilot of the Falcon could see. He sent a radio message to the Coast Guard station at Cape Cod, to tell them of the position of the H-60's crew.

Twenty minutes later the rescue helicopter arrived. But the situation was now very serious. The waves were huge and

78

the wind was blowing at about 100 knots. It was impossible for the pilot of the H-3 to drop a rescue basket into sea as rough as this. The pilot tried again and again, but every time he dropped the basket, it blew straight back towards the helicopter.

The H-3 would soon use up all its fuel. If it stayed near the men any longer, it would crash into the sea too. The pilot had to return the shore. As he turned the helicopter away, he called the *Tamaroa* on his radio. He gave her commander the exact position of the four National Guardsmen.

The four men in the water watched the helicopter disappear into the dark night. They felt terrible. They were cold and tired. They no longer had any hope of rescue and they knew they couldn't stay alive for much longer. Then suddenly, they saw lights rising and falling in the darkness, a few miles from them.

The men from the H-60 had seen the lights of the *Tamaroa,* moving slowly through the huge waves. Soon she was very close to them and Lawrence Brudnicki ordered his crew to slow the ship's engines. He had to decide what was the safest way of rescuing the men in the water. It was going to be very difficult.

The waves were so violent that the four men in the water were getting lifted high into the air. Sometimes a man was taken right to the top of a wave, 30 feet higher than the *Tamaroa*'s deck. At any moment, the men might crash against the side of the ship and be killed.

"It's impossible to throw them a rope in these terrible waves," thought Brudnicki. "The wind will blow the rope away from them. They'll never catch it. And I won't put a rescue swimmer into the water because I might not get him back. There's only one possible way to save these men. They will have to swim to us. We'll put a net over the side of the ship."

The crew of the Tamaroa pushed a very large net over the side of the ship. The net was made of strong rope and it was held by six or seven men on the deck. The men in the water would have to swim to the rope net, then climb up it.

"Swim!" screamed the crew of the *Tamaroa*. "Swim towards us!"

Graham Buschor and John Spillane fought their way through the waves and got to the rope net. They climbed it slowly, but at last they were safely on board the cutter. But the rescue was very difficult and dangerous, not just for the men in the sea, but also for the crew of the *Tamaroa*. All the time that they were holding the rope net for the National Guardsmen to climb, huge waves were crashing down on the deck of the ship and covering the cutter's crew with water.

"It was the most difficult decision of my life," Commander Brudnicki said later. "I had to send my crew out onto that deck, but I knew that I could lose some of them! They could easily be swept into the sea. But I couldn't say, 'I'm just going to let those men die in the sea.' How could I say that?"

Two men were still in the water, and one of them—Jim Mioli—was very weak and tired. He was extremely cold and his hands couldn't hold the ropes. Dave Ruvola tried to hold him up, but Jim kept slipping back into the water.

"You have to climb that net!" Dave screamed. "This is your last chance. If you don't climb it, you'll die, Jim! You have to try!"

The exhausted man nodded. He grabbed the rope net again, and this time he held on to it. Very slowly, the two

They climbed the rope net slowly.

men pulled themselves up to the top of the net, where the *Tamaroa*'s crew could reach them. A moment later, they were safe on the deck of the cutter.

So four men were safe, but the fifth man, Rick Smith, was still missing. He was somewhere out in the terrible darkness of the ocean, lost among the mountainous waves.

Rick Smith was very healthy and he was a very experienced swimmer. The Coast Guard knew exactly where he had jumped into the sea from the helicopter. They sent more planes to look for him.

The Coast Guard searched for Rick Smith for nine days, but they never found him. Finally, they stopped the search. They knew that Rick Smith must be dead.

10

The Search for the Andrea Gail

Most of the swordfishing fleet was far to the east of the storm when it began, so they escaped the worst part of it. The storm still did terrible damage to some of the boats. It destroyed their antennas and their fishing gear. Many of them had to abandon their fishing trips. Their captains had to get back to port as quickly as possible. They needed to repair their boats.

But the only boat that disappeared forever was the *Andrea Gail*.

Chris Cotter, Bobby Shatford's girlfriend, had a strange dream the night after the boat disappeared.

"I dreamed that I was on the *Andrea Gail*," Chris said later. "The weather was stormy and the sea was very rough and gray. The boat was rolling terribly from side to side. I was walking around the *Andrea Gail*, screaming, 'Bobby! Bobby!' But Bobby didn't reply. Then I went down to the fish hold. It was very dark and there was a lot of green seaweed down there. I screamed Bobby's name again but I couldn't find him. Finally I looked down and saw an arm among the green seaweed. It was Bobby's arm. I grabbed him, but I knew that he was dead. And then I woke up."

It was the morning of Wednesday, October 30th. Nobody had heard anything from the *Andrea Gail* for more than thirty-six hours.

Chris lay in bed for a long time that morning, trying to forget about her bad dream. When she got up, she went to sit at her kitchen table. She could see the cold, gray ocean from her window. She watched the waves crashing against the shore. As she watched, the waves were getting larger and stronger.

Gloucester was a few hundred miles away from the center of the storm, so nobody in the town knew how bad the storm was out at sea. Chris had not seen anything about a storm on the TV news. Now she sat smoking one cigarette after another, watching the sea.

As she was sitting there, Susan Brown knocked at the door. Susan was the wife of Bob Brown, the owner of the *Andrea Gail*. Chris knew immediately that something was wrong. Susan was uncomfortable. She kept looking around the room, and she couldn't look at Chris's eyes.

"Listen, Chris," said Susan at last. "I've got some bad news. I don't know how to tell you this, but we can't get in touch[74] with the *Andrea Gail*."

Chris thought about her dream and remembered the dark fish hold, full of seaweed. "He's dead," she thought. "Bobby is dead. I know that."

"We're still trying to get through to Billy Tyne on the radio," Susan continued. "The *Andrea Gail* has probably lost her antennas. I'm sure that she's OK."

Chris didn't really believe this, but she didn't say anything about her dream to Susan.

As soon as Susan had gone, Chris got into her car and drove to the Crow's Nest. It was only ten o'clock in the morning, but there were lots of people there. They were drinking beer and waiting for news. Bobby's mother Ethel, his sisters and brothers, and many other fishermen were in the bar. Everybody looked shocked and upset.

There was a TV in the bar. Everyone watched a news

story about the *Andrea Gail*—a fishing boat that was out of touch with the shore. Terrible pictures kept coming into Chris's mind. She kept imagining Bobby and the crew during their last moments alive.

One person who was not at the Crow's Nest was Bob Brown. He was at home, trying to get in touch with Billy Tyne on his radio. He kept trying to call Linda Greenlaw on the *Hannah Boden* too. But neither of the captains replied. Bob was getting more and more worried.

"Have I lost both the *Andrea Gail* and the *Hannah Boden?*" he asked himself.

Bob called and called all day. At last, in the afternoon, Linda Greenlaw's voice came through on the radio. But it was not clear, so it was difficult for Bob to understand her words.

"I haven't been able to get in touch with Billy for two days!" Linda shouted into the radio. "I'm very worried about the *Andrea Gail!*"

"Yes, I'm worried too," replied Bob Brown. "Keep trying to call him."

At 6 p.m. Bob Brown tried to call the *Andrea Gail* again, but Billy Tyne still didn't reply. Linda Greenlaw hadn't been able to contact him either, nor had any other boat. So at 6:15 p.m. Bob Brown called the Coast Guard and reported that the *Andrea Gail* was missing.

"I think that something terrible might have happened to the boat," he said.

"Nobody has received any Mayday calls from her and there have been no signals from her EPIRB," the Coast Guard told Bob. "So maybe the crew is still OK. Maybe the boat has just lost her antennas and Billy can't call anybody."

Later on the night of Wednesday, October 30th, the Coast Guard called all the other boats near Sable Island on the radio. They asked these boats to try and get in touch with the *Andrea Gail*.

Now there were six boats calling the *Andrea Gail*, but she still didn't answer.

The Coast Guard asked Bob Brown for the names of the crew who were working on the *Andrea Gail*. Bob Brown didn't know for sure—it had been Billy Tyne's job to hire the crew. But soon after, the Coast Guard got a call from a Florida fisherman called Doug Kosco.

"I was going to fish with the *Andrea Gail*," he told them. "But I told Billy that I didn't want to go on this trip. I don't know if Billy found anyone to replace me. I know the other men who went—they were Bugsy Moran, Bobby Shatford, Dale Murphy, and Alfred Pierre."

But there was something that Doug Kosco didn't know. When he had refused to go on the trip, Billy Tyne had called Adam Randall and asked him if he wanted the job. Adam had said yes, so Billy had told him to drive up to Gloucester. But when Adam Randall walked around the *Andrea Gail*, he changed his mind about going on the trip. So then, an hour before the trip, Billy had called Sully, and Sully had agreed to go with him.

On October 30th, Adam Randall was watching the news on TV at home with his girlfriend. Suddenly he saw a report about a missing boat somewhere east of Sable Island. The name of the boat was the *Andrea Gail*. Adam sat up straight.

"That was my boat," he said to his girlfriend.

"What do you mean?" she asked.

"I was going to take a fishing trip on that boat," he replied. "Do you remember when I went up to Gloucester with my father-in-law? Billy Tyne asked me to go on a month's trip on the *Andrea Gail.*

"But when I walked around the deck, I felt a cold wind blowing on my skin. I knew that the boat would never come back and I got off her quickly."

———

A huge search began for the *Andrea Gail.* But it was difficult to look for her because nobody knew exactly where she had sunk. They only knew that she had gone down somewhere in the Atlantic Ocean, east of Sable Island.

The Coast Guard sent fifteen airplanes to look for her, but none of them found anything. Then on November 1st, Albert Johnston, the captain of the *Mary T,* was heading for home. As he was passing about 100 miles to the southwest of Sable Island, he saw some blue fuel drums floating in the ocean. The drums had the letters "AG" painted on their sides.

A few miles further on, Johnston found a second group of drums, then a third group. He called the Coast Guard and told them the position of the drums.

"But the drums don't mean that the *Andrea Gail* has sunk," he thought. "Maybe they were swept off her deck during the storm."

The American and Canadian Coast Guards continued to search, but still they couldn't find the *Andrea Gail.* Then, on November 4th, a Canadian Coast Guard boat found a fuel tank in the sea near Sable Island. It had the name *Andrea Gail* painted on its side.

The following day, in the afternoon, an EPIRB with the number 986 was found on the shore of Sable Island. It was the *Andrea Gail*'s EPIRB, but the Coast Guard said that its sensor had been switched off. This meant that when it had touched the water, the machine wouldn't have worked. It couldn't have sent a signal which would have told the Coast Guard that the *Andrea Gail* was in trouble.

Nobody who knew Billy Tyne—Bob Brown, Linda Greenlaw, Albert Johnston, or anybody else—could explain why the sensor of the EPIRB hadn't been switched on. They couldn't understand it.

Then a rumor[75] started going around Gloucester. People heard another story about the *Andrea Gail*'s EPIRB. This story said that the sensor *had* been switched on, and that the Canadian Coast Guard had received a signal from it. But the Coast Guard didn't want to send rescuers to the *Andrea Gail* in that terrible storm, because it was too dangerous. The rumor said that the Coast Guard told everyone that they had never received an EPIRB signal. And when they found the EPIRB, one of the Coast Guard boat crew switched off the sensor himself. But all this was only a rumor.

Nobody can ever know for sure what happened to the *Andrea Gail*'s EPIRB. It will always be a mystery.

———

On November 6th, a Canadian pilot saw a life raft just off the coast of Nova Scotia. But there was nobody inside it. Two days later, the *Hannah Boden* was sailing back to Gloucester after three weeks at sea, when the crew saw another group of fuel drums floating on the water. These drums had "AG" painted on the sides too.

Finally, just before midnight on November 8th, the Coast Guard stopped the search for the *Andrea Gail*. The fishing boat had been missing for almost two weeks. Planes had searched 116,000 square miles[76] of ocean without finding anyone from the *Andrea Gail*.

The crew saw another group of fuel drums floating on the water.
These drums had "AG" painted on the sides too.

11

Dreams of the Dead

After the search for the *Andrea Gail* ended, Chris Cotter, Bobby Shatford's girlfriend, spent a lot of time alone at the harbor. She waited at the pier, where the fishing boats came in. She stood there, staring at the sea and thinking. She kept thinking about what had happened to the six men on the boat. She kept seeing pictures of their dead bodies in her mind.

A few days later, there was a memorial service[77] in St Ann's Church, close to the Crow's Nest, for the six missing fishermen.

At the church service, Mary Anne Shatford and one of Bobby's brothers read a poem about fishing. Some of Billy Tyne's family, and Sully's brother made speeches[78] too. Bob Brown and his wife, Susan, were also at the memorial service, but they didn't say very much to anybody. And nobody said much to them. This was the third time that men had died on one of Bob Brown's boats. It wasn't his fault, but nobody could forget it.

These were difficult times for the families and friends of the men of the *Andrea Gail*. Everybody knew that the men were dead, but no bodies had been found. It was as if they had not really died, but had only disappeared. So the families could not say goodbye to them.

Debra Murphy, Murph's ex-wife, had a strange dream the night before she heard that the *Andrea Gail* was missing.

"Murph had promised that he would come home in time

She waited at the pier, where the fishing boats came in.

for my birthday at the beginning of November," she said later. "He'd promised to take me out to dinner. Then, on the night of October 29th, he appeared in my dream. He said, 'I'm sorry, I'm not going to get there this time.' When I woke up, the phone was ringing. It was Billy Tyne's girlfriend. She told me that there was a big storm over the Grand Banks and that nobody could get in touch with the *Andrea Gail*."

Later, Debra had called Bob Brown and he'd told her that the Coast Guard had started to search for the boat. But ten days after this, when there was still no news, Debra's son began to ask questions about his father.

"When is Daddy coming back?" asked Dale.

"He's fishing, Dale," answered Debra sadly. "He's fishing in Heaven."

But Dale didn't understand. He knew that his father fished in lots of different places—Hawaii, Puerto Rico, Massachusetts. Was Heaven just another place where his father fished?

"Well, when is he coming back from Heaven?" the boy asked.

Two months later, Dale woke up in the middle of the night, screaming. Terrified, Debra rushed into his room.

"What's wrong, Dale, what's wrong?" she asked him.

"Daddy was in the room," answered Dale. "Daddy was just here."

"What do you mean?" asked Debra.

"Daddy was here and he told me what happened on the boat," the boy answered. "The boat rolled over and Daddy's shirt got caught on a hook. He couldn't free himself and he was pulled under the water."

Debra was surprised and frightened. How could a little boy

know about such things? Had Murph's ghost really been in the room?

Debra went on dreaming about Murph too. She often dreamed that she saw him and ran up to him.

"Where have you been?" she always asked him.

But Murph never answered. Then she always woke up, remembering that he was dead.

———

Chris Cotter had dreams about Bobby Shatford. She dreamed several times that Bobby was standing in front of her. He was always smiling.

"Hey, Bobby, where have you been?" she asked him in her dreams.

But Bobby never answered that question. He just continued smiling. Then he said, "Remember, Christina, that I'll always love you." After that, he disappeared. Every time that Bobby disappeared, he looked very happy, so Chris knew that he was OK.

But Chris herself was *not* OK. Sometimes she went down to the harbor and stood there, waiting for the *Andrea Gail* to come home. At other times, she told her friends that Bobby was coming home.

"Bobby's coming home tonight, I know it," she said.

Chris went out with other men and she tried hard to continue with her life. But she couldn't really believe that Bobby was dead. No one had found his body!

"Maybe Bobby and the others are sitting safely on an island somewhere, looking at the sun on the water," thought Chris.

One night, Chris dreamed that Bobby was living below the sea with a beautiful blonde woman. This person was a mermaid—a woman with the tail of a fish—and Bobby was *her* boyfriend now. Chris woke up, and went straight to the Crow's Nest.

———

About a year after the *Andrea Gail* disappeared, a stranger came into the Crow's Nest and ordered a beer. All the customers in the bar stopped drinking and they stared at him. The man looked exactly like Bobby Shatford.

"You look like my son who died last year," Ethel Shatford explained to the man. "That's why everybody is staring at you."

She showed the man a photo of Bobby and he was very surprised.

"If I sent this photo home to my mother, she would think that it's a photo of me," the man said. "She wouldn't be able to tell the difference between your son and me."

———

People who work at sea often have strange beliefs. They believe that some people are marked, and that it is their destiny[79] to die at sea. Maybe they will escape death several times, but one day the sea will kill them.

Murph *did* believe that he was marked. Before he went on the *Andrea Gail*'s last fishing trip, he told his mother that he would die at sea. In the past, he'd had a few accidents but he'd always had lucky escapes. He finally died on the *Andrea Gail*.

People don't always know that they are marked. Adam Randall was marked and he *didn't* know it. Adam could feel things that nobody else could feel. When he'd walked around the *Andrea Gail*, he'd known that she would never return. He'd known that all her crew would die on the trip. So he got

94

off her quickly. He'd been lucky that time.

After the *Andrea Gail* sank, Adam Randall took a job on Albert Johnston's boat, the *Mary T*. He worked on the *Mary T* for several months, but then she needed some repairs. So Adam had to find a job on another boat. He took a job on a tuna fishing boat called the *Terri Lei*. She was a big, powerful boat with a very experienced crew.

The night before the *Terri Lei* left port, Adam's girlfriend spoke to him on the phone.

"I'm worried about you," she said. "Your voice sounds strange. Is something wrong?"

"No, I'm fine," Adam replied. "I don't really want to go on this trip. But it will be OK. Maybe I'll make a lot of money."

It was spring when the *Terri Lei* headed out to sea, to the warm waters of the Gulf Stream. There were large numbers of tuna fish in the area. Everybody thought that the *Terri Lei* would have a very successful trip.

On the night of April 6th, Adam Randall called his girl-friend from the ship's radio, and they had a half-hour conversation.

"We had some bad weather, but it passed," Adam said. "Everything's looking good now. Our fishing lines are in the water, and we're getting ready for a big catch of tuna tomorrow morning."

"I'm glad that everything's OK," said his girlfriend. "That's good!"

"Yes," Adam said. "But sometimes I can feel ghosts all around the boat. They're the ghosts of men who died at sea. And these fishermen are not at peace. They want to come into the boat."

Early the next morning, the crew of the *Terri Lei* started

hauling in their fishing lines. The weather was a little rough and the waves were high, but it was not a bad storm. The *Terri Lei* was about 135 miles from the shore, and there were lots of other boats in the area.

At about 8:45 a.m. the Coast Guard received a distress signal from a boat's EPIRB. They knew that a boat was in trouble and that it needed help. They were surprised, because the weather wasn't bad. No captain had called on the radio to report any problems, so perhaps the EPIRB signal had been sent by mistake. But it was the Coast Guard's job to find out what was wrong. They sent two rescue planes and a ship to find the boat whose EPIRB had sent the signal.

The planes and the ship followed the EPIRB's signal. At last they saw the machine floating in the water, together with some other gear from a fishing boat. A short distance away there was a life raft with a cover over it. On the side of the raft was painted the name *Terri Lei*.

The *Terri Lei* herself could not be seen and nobody was signaling from the life raft. A rescue swimmer jumped into the sea from the ship. He swam to the raft, to find out what had happened. He looked inside the cover. The raft was empty.

The *Terri Lei* had sunk and nobody had escaped from her.

Adam Randall was dead.

POINTS
FOR
UNDERSTANDING
and
GLOSSARY

Points for Understanding

1

1 The author tells us that the ocean in Gloucester is not very romantic. What does this mean? If it *was* romantic, describe how it might be.
2 At the start of the story, Bobby Shatford has been working on swordfishing boats for less than two months. Why has he started to do this work now?

2

1 Swordfishermen put "lightsticks" on the "gangions" which are attached to their mainline. What are lightsticks and why are they used?
2 On September 20th, when the story begins, Billy Tyne has had a lot of problems. Who is Billy Tyne and what problems has he had?

3

Sully and Billy ask Bobby and Chris whether they will really be OK—Sully asks this twice. Why are people worried about them?

4

1 What does "being on watch" mean?
2 When Albert Johnston hears Billy's radio message about the 30-foot wave, he thinks that there must be something wrong with the *Andrea Gail*. What have we learned earlier in the chapter which helps us to understand why he is worried?
3 Why does Billy Tyne want to take the *Andrea Gail* to the Flemish Cap?

5

1 When the ice machine stops working properly, Billy decides to stay at the fishing grounds for longer. Explain why he decides this. Billy will also have to tell the crew to prepare the mainline in a different way. Guess what these changes are.

2 Why does Billy Tyne want to get back to Gloucester before the other fishing boats?

3 At 3:15 p.m. on October 27th, Billy Tyne calls the Canadian Coast Guard on his radio. Why does he have to do this?

6

1 Bob Case knows that the perfect storm is going to happen before it does happen. Explain why he is sure about this.

2 Why is the information that is received from data buoy 44139 important in this story?

3 Ray Leonard changes his mind about something, and this puts the *Satori* in great danger. What has he changed his mind about?

7

1 The author guesses that the storm might have destroyed the *Andrea Gail*'s radio antennas and its radar. He says that, if this happened, sailing the boat would have been like sailing in the nineteenth century. Explain what he means.

2 Why is it strange that no signal was ever received from the *Andrea Gail*'s EPIRB?

8

1 When seawater pours into the *Satori*, Karen wants the crew to abandon the yacht. But she soon finds out that they cannot do this. Why not?

2 The plan to rescue the crew of the *Satori* has to be changed. What is the first plan? What is the second plan? Why is the change necessary?

9

The crew of the H-60 helicopter is rescued from the sea by the *Tamaroa*. The crew is not rescued by the Coast Guard's H-3. Why is this?

10

1 Doug Kosco gives the Coast Guard the names of some of the men on the *Andrea Gail*. Why is the Coast Guard searching for this information? What information is Doug unable to give them?
2 The Coast Guard searches for the *Andrea Gail*, but other people also find clues which tell them that something terrible has happened to the fishing boat. What clues are found, and who finds them?

11

What has happened to the *Terri Lei*? Make a guess.

Glossary

(*Note*: boats and ships are usually called "she" or "her" when you are talking about them.)

1 **caught in**—*to be caught in a storm* (page 12)
   you use the expression *caught in* when you talk about being outside in bad weather from which you cannot shelter or escape. You don't use the expression "caught by."

2 **meteorologists** (page 12)
   scientists who study the weather and collect information about the air around the Earth. The air is called the *atmosphere*. Meteorologists collect information about the temperature of the air in many places, and about the speed of the winds in many places. They collect information about the movements of warm and cold air in different places, and about the clouds that are covering the Earth in different places. Then they make *forecasts*—they guess what the weather is going to do next.

3 **pier** (page 13)
   a long platform which is built out into the sea from the shore. Ships and boats can be tied to each side of the pier while they are being loaded and unloaded.

4 **Crow's Nest** (page 13)
   on large sailing ships many years ago, there was a small platform near the top of the tallest mast. This platform was called the *crow's nest*. A man stood on this platform and looked at the sea all around the ship. He looked for other ships or for land. This platform, high on the mast, looked a little like a bird's nest in a tree. And that is how it got its name. A crow is a large bird which nests high up in trees. Sailors usually enjoyed spending time in the crow's nest, away from all the other people on the boat and away from the hard work that the others had to do. The expression, "a crow's nest," was sometimes used to mean "a place where a sailor is happy and comfortable." This is why inns in harbor towns are sometimes called The Crow's Nest.

5 **divorce**—*getting a divorce* (page 14)
   when a married couple want to end their marriage, they *get a divorce*. This means that a judge in a law court thinks about why the marriage

has failed and then agrees that the marriage can end. The judge makes a decision about how much of their property and money each person will keep. The judge also makes a decision about who will take care of any young children that the couple have.

6   **back to sea**—*to go back to sea* (page 14)
when a boat leaves its port to travel on the sea, you say that it is *leaving port* and *going to sea*. You leave out the definite article "the" in these expressions. When a boat is going on another trip after a short stay *in port*, you say that it is *going back to sea*. You use these expressions about the sailors on a boat too.

7   **head out**—*going to head out* (page 14)
the verb *head* is often used in expressions which are connected with navigation—decisions about the direction of movement. *Head* simply means "go," "move," or "travel," but it is always joined by a word or some words which tell you about the direction of the movement. You can say that a boat is *heading north, heading south,* and so on. The verb is also used in expressions such as *head out to sea, head back to port, head towards the coast.*

8   **fishing grounds** (page 14)
an area of sea where there are usually many fish. Fishing boats travel to these areas to catch fish.

9   **nickname** (page 15)
a name which your friends and family call you which is not your real name. Sometimes nicknames are shortened forms of real names, but this is not always true. In this book, the nickname "Sully" is a short form of "Sullivan," but the nickname "Bugsy" is not a short form of anything. Many common first names have forms which are not usually called nicknames. For example, Bob or Bobby for Robert, Dick for Richard, Billy for William, Harry for Henry, Jack for John.

10 **shopping center** (page 15)
a place where there are a number of stores of different kinds close together. Sometimes these stores are in a single large building. This is not the same as a *supermarket*, which is a single large store that sells food and many other things. Shopping centers often contain supermarkets. When people buy goods in a supermarket, they take a *shopping cart*—a large metal basket on wheels—around the store. They put all the things they are going to buy into this cart. The carts belong to the supermarket, not to the shoppers.

103

11 *separated* (page 18)

if a husband and wife no longer live together, but they are not divorced, they are *separated*.

12 **child support** (page 18)

if a couple who are separated or divorced have young children, and the young children live with one parent, the other parent usually pays some money every month to the parent who takes care of the children. This money is spent on the children and it is called a *child support* payment.

13 **hired**—*to hire a lawyer* (page 18)

if you pay someone to do a job for you, you *hire* that person.

14 **hurricane** (page 19)

a kind of very bad storm, with strong winds and heavy rain. During a hurricane, winds blow at more than 75 m.p.h. (miles per hour).

15 **Weather Channel** (page 19)

a television channel which only sends out programs about the weather.

16 **monofilament line** (page 21)

a kind of string, that is made from a single piece of *synthetic*, or *man-made* material. Monofilament fishing lines are very strong.

17 **lightstick** (page 21)

lightsticks are clear plastic tubes which give out light. The plastic tube has a chemical inside it and it also has a smaller tube made of glass inside it. This glass tube contains a different chemical. The plastic tube is *sealed* so that no air or water can get into it. To start the light, you bend the plastic tube so that the glass tube inside it breaks. The two chemicals are mixed together and this is what makes the light. Lightsticks will give light for several hours.

18 **haul**—*to haul* (page 22)

to pull strongly.

19 **fish hold** (page 22)

the area below the deck on a fishing boat where the fish which have been caught are stored.

20 **fishcakes** (page 24)

a kind of food made of small pieces of fish and potato, which are mixed together. This mixture is shaped into small cakes, and then cooked.

21 **glared**—*to glare at somebody* (page 26)

to look angrily at someone.

22 **mood**—*to be in a bad mood* (page 27)
   if you are unhappy and angry with the people around you, or with
   yourself, you are *in a bad mood*. If you are happy, you are *in a good
   mood*.

23 **father-in-law** (page 28)
   the father of the person you are married to.

24 **mind**—*to make up your own mind* (page 28)
   to make a decision about something without help from anybody
   else.

25 **reputation** (page 28)
   if lots of people say the same thing about the way you usually
   behave, or the things that you do, that is your *reputation*. For example, you could have a reputation for being good at driving a car, or
   you could have a reputation for being rude to people.

26 **frozen pizzas** (page 30)
   a *pizza* is a kind of flat Italian bread cooked with vegetables and
   cheese, and sometimes also meat or fish, on top of it. Frozen pizzas
   are stored in a refrigerator until you want to cook them.

27 **checkout counters** (page 30)
   a *checkout counter* is a place in a supermarket where you pay for all
   the things you are buying. The person who operates the checkout
   counter enters into a computer the separate costs of everything in
   your shopping cart. Then the computer gives the total cost of all
   the things that you are buying.

28 **galley** (page 32)
   the kitchen of a boat or a ship.

29 **whaleback deck** (page 32)
   a raised area of the deck on a boat or ship which is rounded, like
   the back of a whale. This shape allows water which gets onto the
   boat in bad weather to run off the deck quickly.

30 **VCR** (page 34)
   Video Cassette Recorder—a machine which makes recordings from
   a television onto video tape in a cassette. A VCR also plays video
   tapes of movies.

31 **steel plates** (page 38)
   flat pieces of steel.

32 **horsepower** (page 38)
   a measurement of power. It is used to describe the power of engines.
   One horsepower is the amount of power needed to raise a weight of
   550 pounds a distance of one foot, in one second.

33 *knots* (page 38)

a knot is a measurement of speed at sea. If you travel at *one knot*, you are traveling at a speed of one nautical mile in an hour. One nautical mile = 1.1508 land miles.

34 *inspected*—*to inspect something* (page 39)

to look at something very carefully, and check that it is safe and correct.

35 *cope with*—*to cope with something* (page 39)

when something bad happens and a person or a machine keeps control of what is happening, they are *coping with* this thing.

36 **Canadian national water**s (page 39)

a country which has a coast has *national waters*. This is the area of sea nearest to its coast. This sea belongs to that country and is controlled by it. Sea further from the coast is not controlled by any country, and is called *international waters*. Note: the plural of *water* is always used in these expressions. A country's national waters are sometimes called its *territorial waters*—waters which are part of its territory.

37 **helm, radar, and navigational instruments** (page 40)

the *helm* of a ship is the wheel which you turn to steer it. The *radar* is a machine which uses *radio waves* to show the positions of any objects which are nearby, e.g. other ships. Their positions are shown on a screen like a television screen. Other *navigational instruments* include the *compass*, which tells the captain the exact direction the ship is traveling in.

38 *set the course*—*to set a course* (page 40)

when the captain of a ship or plane decides on the direction they want to travel in, they *set a course*. They steer the ship or plane in that direction. When they change direction, they are *setting a new course*. A course is usually described using the *points of the compass*— you can set a course of north northeast, or a course of twenty-nine degrees west. (See also Glossary Number 48).

39 *autopilot* (page 40)

a machine which steers a boat or a plane to keep it on the course which has been set.

40 *bunks* (page 41)

the beds on a boat or a ship.

41 *weather systems* (page 41)

things like areas of hot and cold air, and moving clouds of rain, combine to make *weather systems*.

42 **blow hard** (page 42)

a wind—air that is moving quickly—is described as *blowing*. When it is moving very strongly it is described as *blowing hard*.

43 **foam** (page 42)

groups of tiny bubbles of air which stick together on the surface of sea water. This *foam* usually looks white.

44 **fishing charts** (page 44)

charts are maps of parts of seas or rivers. They show the depth of the water as well as the shape of any nearby land. Fishing charts give fishermen information about the area of water where large numbers of fish are found.

45 **pumped**—*to pump* (page 47)

a machine which moves liquid from one place to another is called a *pump*. If you use a pump to move liquid, you are *pumping* it.

46 **fishing gear** (page 49)

all the equipment used for fishing—the lines, clips, hooks, nets etc.

47 **Canadian Coast Guard** (page 51)

most countries which have sea coasts have a *coast guard*. This is a group of people who watch and defend the coast. They work like a police force inside a country's *national waters* (See Glossary Number 36). The members of this group—*coast guardsmen*—stop people from breaking the law. For example, they stop people bringing things or people into the country without permission. They also help people who get into danger at sea. Both the Canadian Coast Guard and the U.S. Coast Guard appear in this story.

48 **44:25 degrees north, 49:05 degrees west** (page 52)

[Say: "Forty-four, twenty-five degrees north. Forty-nine, zero-five degrees west."]

These are *co-ordinates* which, when they are combined, show an exact position on a map. A *degree* is a measurement of part of a circle. There are 360 degrees in a circle. Each degree is divided into 60 *minutes*. Maps are marked with horizontal lines, called *lines of latitude* and vertical lines called *lines of longitude*. Degrees of latitude are given as *north* or *south* of a line around the middle of the Earth. Degrees of longitude are given as *east* or *west* of a line running from the North Pole to the South Pole of the Earth. See the maps on pages 5 and 6.

49 *fax of a weather chart* (page 53)

fax—the word is a short form of the word *facsimile*. A fax is an exact picture of something which is sent by radio transmission or through a phone line. A fax can be a picture of another picture—a map, for example—or it can be a picture of a page of words—a message. A *weather chart* is a map which shows weather systems.

50 *front of cold air* (page 53)

the place where two bodies of air meet is called a *front*. One body of air is always warmer than the other. Where cold air replaces warm air, the front is called a *cold front*. Where warm air replaces cold air, the front is called a *warm front*.

51 *path—the path of a storm* (page 55)

the area over which a storm travels is called its *path*. The word is also used for the area which a storm is about to travel over.

52 *engine room* (page 56)

the place below the deck of a ship or a large boat where the engine is fixed.

53 *fire alarm and high-water alarm* (page 56)

alarms are signals which tell you when you are in danger. Some alarms are visual—they have brightly flashing lights. Some alarms are audible—they have bells or sirens that make a loud noise. A *high-water alarm* tells the captain that too much water is getting into his boat.

54 *emergency lighting* (page 56)

in a large boat or ship, the electricity for most of the lights is made by a machine which is driven by the engine. If the engine stops because it has broken, these lights go off, but some other lights come on at the same time. They are the *emergency lights*. They are powered by a battery and they will work for several hours.

55 **U.S. National Weather Service** (page 56)

this is part of the National Oceanic and Atmospheric Administration—the NOAA. Meteorologists (see Glossary Number 2) work for the Weather Service and their forecasts are used by any Americans who need to know about the weather.

56 *satellite photos* (page 56)

photos of the Earth taken from satellites—machines which circle the earth at a great height. *Satellite photos* show areas of cloud, and other weather systems, and meteorologists use the information from them to make weather forecasts.

57 **bounce off**—*to bounce off* (page 57)

if a moving object meets another, heavier object which is moving in the opposite direction or standing still, the lighter object *bounces off* the heavier one. The lighter object stops its forward movement and moves backwards. When two objects meet in this way, the meeting is called a *collision*—the two objects *collide*.

58 **misty** (page 62)

when the weather is *misty*, there are large numbers of tiny drops of water in the air near the ground or the sea. It is difficult to see through this pale gray *mist*.

59 **shipping lanes** (page 63)

shipping lanes are like roads through the sea. Large ships stay in these lanes when they are traveling from one place to another.

60 **safety lines** (page 63)

ropes or cords which people use when working on the deck of a boat in bad weather. One end of the line is fixed to the boat and the other end to a person's body. Then if the sea washes the person off the boat, the person can pull him or herself back onto the deck.

61 **serious situation** (page 64)

if things are going badly for you, or you are in danger, you are in a *serious situation*.

62 **radio antennas** (page 64)

an *antenna* is a thin metal rod through which radio signals are sent and received. Sometimes the plural word *antennae* is used, although this is usually found in British English, not in American English.

63 **currents** (page 65)

when the water in a river or the sea moves strongly in one direction, this is called a *current*.

64 **distress signal** (page 66)

if a boat or a plane is in trouble and it is going to sink or crash, it is *in distress*. At this time, emergency equipment is used to send out a *distress signal*. Other boats and planes, and coast guard stations will receive this signal, and they will start searching for the people from the boat or plane that is in distress.

65 **EPIRB** (page 66)

Emergency Position Indicating Radio Beacon. This machine is part of a boat or plane's emergency equipment. It sends out a radio signal—a distress signal—when its sensor touches water. Each machine has its own special radio signal and its exact position in the sea can be found by the equipment used by coast guards.

66 **beat the shark to deat**h—*to beat something or someone to death* (page 67)
to kill something or someone by hitting it or them again and again.

67 *submarine* (page 67)
a boat that can travel under the surface of the water. Submarines are usually warships which carry weapons.

68 *companionway* (page 70)
a stairway on a boat or a ship.

69 *abandon ship*—*to abandon ship* (page 70)
if you leave a boat or ship while it is at sea because you are in danger, you are *abandoning ship*. In this expression you always use the word "ship," no matter what size or kind of boat or ship you are talking about. You leave out the definite article "the", in this expression.

70 *Mayday call* (page 71)
you send a *Mayday call* from your radio if your boat, ship or plane is in great danger. It is a call for help to anyone who is near you. The word "mayday" comes from the second part of the French expression *venez m'aider*, which means "come to help me." The French *m'aider* sounds like the English words "May day".

71 *risking their lives*—*to risk your life* (page 73)
if you do something that is so dangerous that you might be killed, you are *risking your life*.

72 *neoprene wetsuit* (page 75)
neoprene is a kind of very strong, soft material, like rubber. A *wetsuit* is a piece of clothing that covers the whole body of a swimmer. *Swimming fins* are like large flat shoes which help a swimmer move through the water quickly and easily. A *hood* is worn over the head and neck, and a *mask* is worn over the face. A *snorkel* is a curved tube which a swimmer holds in his or her mouth so that he or she can breathe when his or her face is just under the water. See the illustrations on page 9.

73 *National Guard* (page 78)
in the U.S., there is an Army and an Air Force for the whole country. These are called *federal* forces and they work for the federal government. But each state in the U.S. also has some soldiers and airmen who do not work in the federal forces. They work for their state governments. These state forces are called the *National Guard*.

74 **get in touch**—*get in touch with someone* (page 84)
to speak to someone who is far away. You can use this expression
with the name of a boat, when it really means to speak to the
people on that boat.

75 **rumor** (page 88)
if you say something about someone or something without knowing
whether it is true, this is a *rumor*. When many people in a town
are telling each other a rumor, you can say that a rumor is *going
around* that town.

76 **square miles** (page 88)
a square mile is a measurement of the area of a surface. A piece of
land or water which is one mile long and one mile wide has an area
of one square mile.

77 **memorial service** (page 90)
a meeting, usually in a church, at which people remember someone
who has died. This is not the same as a *funeral service*, because the
body of the dead person is not there. In this book, there is one
memorial service for all the six Gloucester fishermen who have
died.

78 **speeches**—*to make a speech* (page 90)
if you talk to all the people who are attending a meeting, a wedding
or a funeral, you are making a *speech*.

79 **destiny** (page 94)
if something is going to happen to you, and you have no control
over it, this thing is your *destiny*.

111

Published by Macmillan Heinemann ELT
Between Towns Road, Oxford OX4 3PP
Macmillan Heinemann ELT is an imprint of
Macmillan Publishers Ltd
Companies and representatives throughout the world

ISBN 0333 99074 9

This retold version by Anne Collins for Macmillan Guided Readers
First published 2003
Text © Macmillan Publishers Limited 2003
Design and illustration © Macmillan Publishers Limited 2003
Heinemann is a registered trademark of Reed Educational and Professional Publishing
Limited
This version first published 2003

Illustrations by Chris Riley
Maps on pages 5 and 6, and the illustration on page 57 by John Gilkes
Cover by Getty and Richard Gillingwater

Printed in China

2009 2008 2007 2006 2005 2004 2003
10   9   8   7   6   5   4   3   2   1